TAXES
are
EASY

The "Tax Cuts & Jobs Act"

TCJA, an Introduction

2018 Tax Law
and Forms

Michael D. Meyer, EA
IRS Enrolled Agent

ISBN-13: 978-0-578-57025-9
Published via Kindle Direct Publishing at: https://kdp.amazon.com/en_US/
1st printing: September 5th, 2019

DEDICATIONS

To my wife Michele of over 32-years who patiently encourages my unreasonable aspirations like to write a book about taxes.

To Martina for the Cover Design

To Michele, Jenn, Eileen and Shereen for always saying "You Can Do It!"

To Jeannette at H&R Block, who taught my first Fall of 2012 tax course, and then recommended me to the tax pros at the 602 10th Ave. office

To my H&R Block tax mentors at 602 10th Ave. in Manhattan
Pat, Albert, Diane, Connie and Matt

To my New York City H&R Block EA tax mentor, Philip, who was instrumental in helping me pass the Enrolled Agent exams

To Frank, an EA at H&R Block at 2013 Williamsbridge Road in the Bronx, who is by far the most amazing tax teacher I have ever learned from

To my New York City Enrolled Agent EA mentors Phyllis & Frank, who also are NTPI Fellows

To my NTPI Fellow teachers Kathy, Thomas and Frank, who are all EAs, NTPI Fellows, and U.S. Tax Court Practitioners, USTCPs

To my TurboTaxLive™ manager Paul, who also is an EA and NTPI Fellow

To the TurboTaxLive™ Slack Lead EAs, CPAs and JDs, who graciously partnered with me during my two years as a TurboTaxLive™ Expert, to help resolve difficult tax law issues with TurboTax™ customers

To my Facebook classmates at our 1978 Lawrenceburg High School group

To the Facebook "The Choose Yourself Publishing Circle" group that was started by James Altucher to teach new authors how to self-publish

To the generous reviewers of this book who provided their Testimonials

TABLE OF CONTENTS

Explanation about the Organization of the Book Chapters

- Each chapter begins with a TOPICS SUMMARY, so you can preview all of the 41 TCJA topics just by reviewing the first few pages of each chapter.
- The first page of each chapter is a right-facing page
- Each topic is explained in full detail within the chapter, often accompanied with an example about the change in the tax law for that topic.
- Most topic explanations have Hyperlinks to web articles, IRS forms, blog posts, etc. to further explain the changes in the tax laws. There are 56 in the book.
- Tax law related words in the text are capitalized for emphasis.

ACRONYMS / DEFINITIONS

Refer to these acronyms / definitions as you read about the topics in the book.

ABLE Account	"Achieving a Better Life Experience" Act of 2014 savings account
AGI	Adjusted Gross Income
AMT	Alternative Minimum Tax
AOTC	American Opportunity Tax Credit
Bonus Depreciation	Additional first-year depreciation deduction of a business asset
CPA	Certified Public Accountant
EA	Enrolled Agent
FHA	Federal Housing Administration
Hyperlink	A clickable, blue underlined link to an Internet web site address
IRA	Individual Retirement Arrangement
IRC	Internal Revenue Code
IRS	Internal Revenue Service
ITIN	Individual Taxpayer Identification Number
IPO	Initial Public Offering
JD	Juris Doctor, the Doctor of Jurisprudence law degree
K-12	Kindergarten through to the 12th grade of High School
KDP	Kindle Direct Publishing, used to publish this book on Amazon
LLC	Lifetime Learning Credit
LLC	Limited Liability Company
MAGI	Modified Adjusted Gross Income
MFJ	Married Filing Jointly filing status
MFS	Married Filing Separately filing status
NAEA	National Association of Enrolled Agents
NTPI Fellow	National Tax Practice Institute™ Fellow
NYSSEA	New York State Society of Enrolled Agents
PDF	Portable Digital Format, often used to save computer documents
PTP	Publicly Traded Partnership
QBI	Qualified Business Income
Quintile	A quintile is one of five values that divide a range of data into five equal parts, each being 1/5th (20 percent) of the range.
REIT	Real Estate Investment Trust
Roth IRA	An IRA that has its distributions not taxed at retirement, but allows no IRA deduction on the Taxpayer's yearly tax return
RSUs	Restricted Stock Units
SALT	State And Local Taxes
Schedule C (Form 1040)	Form used to report your self-employment income and expenses
Section 179 Expense	Expensing a business asset in first year, instead of depreciating
SE Tax	Self-Employment Tax
S-Corp	S-Corporation
SSTB	Specified Service Trade or Business
TCJA	Tax Cuts and Jobs Act
Traditional IRA	An IRA that has its distributions taxed at retirement, but can allow an IRA deduction on the Taxpayer's yearly tax return
TurboTax™	Software to enable a Taxpayer to self-prepare their tax return
UBIA	Unadjusted Basis Immediately after Acquisition
USTCP	United States Tax Court Practitioner
W-2	Form used to report your salary wage information to the IRS
1099 Forms	Forms used to report other types of income information to IRS
529 Plan	Qualified Tuition Program saving plan established by your State

INTRODUCTION

The "Tax Cuts and Jobs Act" TCJA passed by Congress and signed by President Trump on December 22nd, 2017, enacted significant tax law changes that began to affect the 2018 tax year. Many of these changes will continue through to the 2025 tax year. This book explains 41 topics from the TCJA related changes that could have affected your 2018 U.S. Individual Income Tax Return.

I recommend you use this three-step approach to quickly become familiar with many of the 41 TCJA related changes that could have affected your 2018 U.S. Individual Income Tax Return. An hour of your time invested should be sufficient.

1) Review the Table of Contents for an introduction to the 41 TCJA changes
   • This should take about 10-minutes

2) Go to the first page of each chapter to then read the TOPICS SUMMARY that outlines the several topics discussed in that particular chapter.
   • The first page of each chapter is a right-facing page
   • The chapters begin on pages 3, 15, 21, 35, 43, 51, 55, 61 and 81
   • This should take about 20-minutes

3) Flip through the entire book to read and stop at the large, bold, underlined, numbered "Headlines" above each of the 41 topics. This will give you a good idea of how each topic is explained in the text below each "Headline". Then stop and skim-read any topics you find applicable to your tax scenario.
   • This should take about a half-hour to review the 41 "Headlines".

I personally learn new, sometimes complicated Tax Law, best through repetition. That is why I organized the book to present the 41 TCJA related changes in three levels of detail. First in the table of contents, next in the TOPICS SUMMARIES, and lastly in the chapters. This repetition is intended to present the TCJA changes starting with an overview through to the detailed explanations.

Tax law related words in the text are capitalized. I believe this emphasis aids in learning the new tax law terms. That is why I deviated from capitalization rules.

The paperback version of this book has 56 underlined Hyperlinks to articles, websites and IRS tax forms to enhance the topic explanations. Type those web addresses into any Internet browser to see the links. The e-book versions of this book have "live" blue underlined Hyperlinks. Click the links for the references.

The purpose of this book is to give you a very good overview and explanation of 41 of the TCJA related changes that could have affected your 2018 U.S. Individual Income Tax Return. Most TCJA changes affect the 2018 to 2025 tax years.

Chapter 1:

The 2018 Form 1040 postcard and the 2018 Tax Rates

TOPICS SUMMARY #1 to #3

1) <u>The 2018 Form 1040 postcard with its six new supporting Schedules</u>

The three previously used U.S. Individual Income Tax Return forms being the 1040EZ, 1040A and 2-page Form 1040 have been discontinued by the IRS for the tax years 2018 and beyond. The IRS has replaced them with a new single-page 2018 Form 1040 postcard and six new supporting Schedules - for the 2018 tax year.

2) <u>The revised 2018 Individual Income Tax Rate Brackets</u>

The 2018 tax year Individual Income Tax Rate Brackets now use slightly lowered tax rates and slightly higher associated income levels. Most taxpayers will benefit from a lowered tax rate for the 2018 tax year through to the 2025 tax year, adjusted yearly for inflation. The after-tax income of most taxpayers will begin to increase in 2018, meaning you keep more of your income, after taxes.

3) <u>The revised 2018 Capital Gain Tax Rate Schedule</u>

The 2018 Capital Gain Tax Rate Schedule is now calculated differently. The 0%/15%/20% Capital Gain Tax Rate levels are now based on your Filing Status and Taxable Income levels. In recent tax years they were based solely on the Income Tax Rate Brackets. These changes remain in effect through to the 2025 tax year, with the schedule being adjusted yearly for inflation.

1) The new single-page 2018 Form 1040 postcard

The new single-page 2018 Form 1040 postcard can be downloaded at: https://www.irs.gov/pub/irs-pdf/f1040.pdf. It is easier if you print out the full-sized form so you can follow the explanations in this book.

The IRS introduced the draft Form 1040 postcard in June 2018 for review and comment. It is designed to be folded in half and mailed, if you are a taxpayer who still mails in your tax return. The IRS also introduced six new Schedules, numbered 1 to 6, to support this new Form 1040. See the final Form 1040 and six Schedules on the following pages.

The previously used tax forms 1040EZ, 1040A, and 2-page Form 1040 have been discontinued by the IRS. They will not be used for any tax years after the most recently completed 2017 tax year. For the 2018 tax year the new single page Form 1040 postcard will be used.

Only a relatively few number of taxpayers will have such a simple tax scenario that they can mail in the new Form 1040 postcard. Most taxpayers will need to use one or more of the six new Schedules to list their additional sources of Income, Adjustments, Credits, Taxes and Payments. The Schedules must be included with their mailed tax return.

Most taxpayers, about 90% according to the IRS, use tax software to self-prepare and e-file their own tax return, or they hire a Paid Preparer to complete and e-file their tax return.[1] That 90% of the taxpayer population will benefit from updated tax preparation software that will automatically handle the new 2018 Form 1040 and its six Schedules. Software like TurboTax™ will be updated, as well as the professional software every Paid Preparer uses to prepare a Client's tax return.

What will be new is the final PDF copy or paper printout of your 2018 tax year return. Your 2018 tax year information will now be displayed on this new 2018 Form 1040 postcard, along with one or more of the six new supporting Schedules, if your tax scenario requires the Schedules.

Use the images of the 2018 Form 1040 postcard and six Schedules to then follow the line-by-line explanations given on the following pages 6 and 7. Flip backwards and forward between the 2018 Form 1040 postcard and six Schedules as you read the text on pages 6 and 7.

[1] https://www.irs.gov/pub/irs-utl/oc-e-file.pdf

The new 2018 Form 1040 postcard: the Top - page 1

©2019 Internal Revenue Service

Form 1040 Department of the Treasury—Internal Revenue Service (99)
U.S. Individual Income Tax Return **2018** OMB No. 1545-0074 IRS Use Only—Do not write or staple in this space.

Filing status: ☐ Single ☐ Married filing jointly ☐ Married filing separately ☐ Head of household ☐ Qualifying widow(er)

Your first name and initial | Last name | Your social security number

Your standard deduction: ☐ Someone can claim you as a dependent ☐ You were born before January 2, 1954 ☐ You are blind

If joint return, spouse's first name and initial | Last name | Spouse's social security number

Spouse standard deduction: ☐ Someone can claim your spouse as a dependent ☐ Spouse was born before January 2, 1954 ☐ Full-year health care coverage or exempt (see inst.)
☐ Spouse is blind ☐ Spouse itemizes on a separate return or you were dual-status alien

Home address (number and street). If you have a P.O. box, see instructions. | Apt. no. | Presidential Election Campaign (see inst.) ☐ You ☐ Spouse

City, town or post office, state, and ZIP code. If you have a foreign address, attach Schedule 6. | If more than four dependents, see inst. and ✓ here ▶ ☐

Dependents (see instructions):
(1) First name | Last name | (2) Social security number | (3) Relationship to you | (4) ✓ If qualifies for (see inst.): Child tax credit | Credit for other dependents

Sign Here
Joint return?
See instructions.
Keep a copy for your records.

Under penalties of perjury, I declare that I have examined this return and accompanying schedules and statements, and to the best of my knowledge and belief, they are true, correct, and complete. Declaration of preparer (other than taxpayer) is based on all information of which preparer has any knowledge.

Your signature | Date | Your occupation | If the IRS sent you an Identity Protection PIN, enter it here (see inst.)

Spouse's signature. If a joint return, **both** must sign. | Date | Spouse's occupation | If the IRS sent you an Identity Protection PIN, enter it here (see inst.)

Paid Preparer Use Only
Preparer's name | Preparer's signature | PTIN | Firm's EIN | Check if: ☐ 3rd Party Designee
Firm's name ▶ | | Phone no. | ☐ Self-employed
Firm's address ▶

For Disclosure, Privacy Act, and Paperwork Reduction Act Notice, see separate instructions. | Cat. No. 11320B | Form **1040** (2018)

©2019 Internal Revenue Service

The new 2018 Form 1040 postcard: the Bottom - page 2

Form 1040 (2018) — Page **2**

1	Wages, salaries, tips, etc. Attach Form(s) W-2		1	
2a	Tax-exempt interest .	2a		
	b Taxable interest		2b	
3a	Qualified dividends . .	3a		
	b Ordinary dividends		3b	
4a	IRAs, pensions, and annuities .	4a		
	b Taxable amount		4b	
5a	Social security benefits	5a		
	b Taxable amount		5b	
6	Total income. Add lines 1 through 5. Add any amount from Schedule 1, line 22		6	
7	Adjusted gross income. If you have no adjustments to income, enter the amount from line 6; otherwise, subtract Schedule 1, line 36, from line 6		7	
8	Standard deduction or itemized deductions (from Schedule A)		8	
9	Qualified business income deduction (see instructions)		9	
10	Taxable income. Subtract lines 8 and 9 from line 7. If zero or less, enter -0-		10	
11	a Tax (see inst.) _____ (check if any from: 1 ☐ Form(s) 8814 2 ☐ Form 4972 3 ☐ _____) b Add any amount from Schedule 2 and check here . . . . ▶ ☐		11	
12	a Child tax credit/credit for other dependents _____ b Add any amount from Schedule 3 and check here ▶ ☐		12	
13	Subtract line 12 from line 11. If zero or less, enter -0-		13	
14	Other taxes. Attach Schedule 4 .		14	
15	Total tax. Add lines 13 and 14		15	
16	Federal income tax withheld from Forms W-2 and 1099		16	
17	Refundable credits: a EIC (see inst.) _____ b Sch. 8812 _____ c Form 8863 _____ Add any amount from Schedule 5		17	
18	Add lines 16 and 17. These are your total payments		18	
19	If line 18 is more than line 15, subtract line 15 from line 18. This is the amount you **overpaid**		19	
20a	Amount of line 19 you want **refunded to you.** If Form 8888 is attached, check here . . . ▶ ☐		20a	
▶ b	Routing number _____ ▶ c Type: ☐ Checking ☐ Savings			
▶ d	Account number _____			
21	Amount of line 19 you want applied to your 2019 estimated tax . ▶	21		
22	Amount you owe. Subtract line 18 from line 15. For details on how to pay, see instructions . . . ▶		22	
23	Estimated tax penalty (see instructions) . . . . . ▶	23		

Attach Form(s) W-2. Also attach Form(s) W-2G and 1099-R if tax was withheld.

Standard Deduction for—
• Single or married filing separately, $12,000
• Married filing jointly or Qualifying widow(er), $24,000
• Head of household, $18,000
• If you checked any box under Standard deduction, see instructions.

Refund
Direct deposit?
See instructions.

Amount You Owe

Go to www.irs.gov/Form1040 for instructions and the latest information. | Form **1040** (2018)

©2019 Internal Revenue Service

<u>Why did the IRS redesign the 2018 Form 1040?</u>

The Congress and the President wanted to "simplify" the process of filing a tax return down to an "easy to use" 1-page form that can be folded in half and mailed to the IRS. Thus the new 2018 Form 1040 postcard.

In reality all that happened is the IRS had to reshuffle the information shown on 79 lines previously reported on the 2-page Form 1040, and redistribute those 79 lines between the new Form 1040 postcard and its six new supporting Schedules. The six new Schedules actually retain most of the line numbers from the discontinued 2-page Form 1040.

The new 2018 Form 1040 Postcard reports the following to the IRS:

<u>On the new 2018 Form 1040 postcard: the Top - page 1</u>

- Your name, your spouse's name, and the names and relationship to you of any Qualifying Child and/or Qualifying Relative listed on your tax return as a Dependent you support.
- Checkbox to list your Filing Status as:
  - Single, Married Filing Jointly, Married Filing Separately, Head of Household, or as a Qualifying Widow(er) with a Child or Children
- The Social Security numbers of everyone listed on the tax return
  - Or the ITIN numbers (Individual Taxpayer Identification Number)
- The mailing address you want IRS correspondence sent to
- Checkbox if the Taxpayer or Spouse is age 65 or older, blind, or both
- Checkbox if you are claimed as a Dependent on a taxpayer's return
  - For example, you are a Qualifying Child claimed on your parent's tax return as a Dependent, but you made enough wage income with a summer job to be required to file a tax return on your own behalf.
- Checkbox if the Married Filing Separately spouse Itemized Deductions
- Checkbox if your household had full-year health care coverage
- Checkbox to contribute $3 to the Presidential Election Campaign Fund
- Checkboxes to indicate if your Dependents listed on the tax return qualify you for the Child Tax Credit or Credit for Other Dependents
- A section to sign/date the tax return and list your occupation(s). The perjury statement is also here to attest you told the truth to the IRS.
- A section to list your Identity Protection PINs if the IRS issued you this number because of previous identity theft issues you experienced.
- A section to list the name and information for a Paid Preparer if you hired a tax professional to complete and e-file your tax return.

On the new 2018 Form 1040 postcard: the Bottom - page 2

Your Total Income on line 6
- Your Wages, Salaries, Tips, etc. listed on a W-2 form on line 1
- Tax-Exempt Interest and Taxable Interest on lines 2a/2b
- Qualified Dividends and Ordinary Dividends on lines 3a/3b
- Total and Taxable IRAs, Pensions and Annuities on lines 4a/4b
- Total and Taxable Social Security Benefits on lines 5a/5b
- Additional Income amounts added to line 6 from line 22 on Schedule 1

Your Adjusted Gross Income shown on line 7
- Adjustments to Income (line 36 on Schedule 1) subtracted from line 6

Your Standard Deduction or Itemized Deductions shown on line 8
- Standard Deduction values shown in left margin on Form 1040 page 2
- Itemized Deduction categories are totaled on the Schedule A form

The new Qualified Business Income deduction on line 9

Your Taxable Income value shown on line 10

Your Initial Tax Liability shown on line 11
- Using Schedule 2 to calculate some additional types of Taxes

Your Nonrefundable Credits shown on line 12
- The Child Tax Credit and Credit for Other Dependents
- Any other Nonrefundable Credits from Schedule 3

Other Taxes & your Total Tax Liability before payments & credits
- Other taxes from Schedule 4 added to line 13 for Total Tax on line 15

The Federal Income Tax withheld from your W-2 and 1099 forms-line 16

Refundable Credits to reduce Total Tax / increase your refund - line 17
- Earned Income Credit, Additional Child Tax Credit, Education Credits
- Other Payment types and Refundable Credits from Schedule 5

Your Total Payments shown on line 18

Your Refund Amount on line 19 or the Amount you Owe on line 22
- Information for which Bank Account to direct-deposit your refund into

Schedule 6 to list a Foreign Address and/or Third Party Designee

2018 Schedules 1, 2 & 3 - that support the 2018 Form 1040 postcard

SCHEDULE 1 (Form 1040)	**Additional Income and Adjustments to Income**	OMB No. 1545-0074
Department of the Treasury Internal Revenue Service	▶ Attach to Form 1040. ▶ Go to *www.irs.gov/Form1040* for instructions and the latest information.	**2018** Attachment Sequence No. **01**
Name(s) shown on Form 1040		Your social security number

Additional	1–9b	Reserved	**1–9b**	
Income	10	Taxable refunds, credits, or offsets of state and local income taxes	**10**	
	11	Alimony received	**11**	
	12	Business income or (loss). Attach Schedule C or C-EZ . . . . ▶	**12**	
	13	Capital gain or (loss). Attach Schedule D if required. If not required, check here ▶ ☐	**13**	
	14	Other gains or (losses). Attach Form 4797	**14**	
	15a	Reserved	**15b**	
	16a	Reserved	**16b**	
	17	Rental real estate, royalties, partnerships, S corporations, trusts, etc. Attach Schedule E	**17**	
	18	Farm income or (loss). Attach Schedule F	**18**	
	19	Unemployment compensation	**19**	
	20a	Reserved	**20b**	
	21	Other income. List type and amount ▶ _____	**21**	
	22	Combine the amounts in the far right column. If you don't have any adjustments to income, enter here and include on Form 1040, line 6. Otherwise, go to line 23 . .	**22**	
Adjustments	23	Educator expenses	23	
to Income	24	Certain business expenses of reservists, performing artists, and fee-basis government officials. Attach Form 2106 . .	24	
	25	Health savings account deduction. Attach Form 8889 .	25	
	26	Moving expenses for members of the Armed Forces. Attach Form 3903	26	
	27	Deductible part of self-employment tax. Attach Schedule SE	27	
	28	Self-employed SEP, SIMPLE, and qualified plans . . .	28	
	29	Self-employed health insurance deduction	29	
	30	Penalty on early withdrawal of savings	30	
	31a	Alimony paid b Recipient's SSN ▶	31a	
	32	IRA deduction	32	
	33	Student loan interest deduction	33	
	34	Reserved	34	
	35	Reserved	35	
	36	Add lines 23 through 35	**36**	

For Paperwork Reduction Act Notice, see your tax return instructions.   Cat. No. 71479F   Schedule 1 (Form 1040) 2018

©2019 Internal Revenue Service

SCHEDULE 2 (Form 1040)	**Tax**	OMB No. 1545-0074
Department of the Treasury Internal Revenue Service	▶ Attach to Form 1040. ▶ Go to *www.irs.gov/Form1040* for instructions and the latest information.	**2018** Attachment Sequence No. **02**
Name(s) shown on Form 1040		Your social security number

Tax	38–44	Reserved	**38–44**	
	45	Alternative minimum tax. Attach Form 6251	**45**	
	46	Excess advance premium tax credit repayment. Attach Form 8962	**46**	
	47	Add the amounts in the far right column. Enter here and include on Form 1040, line 11	**47**	

For Paperwork Reduction Act Notice, see your tax return instructions.   Cat. No. 71478U   Schedule 2 (Form 1040) 2018

©2019 Internal Revenue Service

SCHEDULE 3 (Form 1040)	**Nonrefundable Credits**	OMB No. 1545-0074
Department of the Treasury Internal Revenue Service	▶ Attach to Form 1040. ▶ Go to *www.irs.gov/Form1040* for instructions and the latest information.	**2018** Attachment Sequence No. **03**
Name(s) shown on Form 1040		Your social security number

Nonrefundable	48	Foreign tax credit. Attach Form 1116 if required	**48**	
Credits	49	Credit for child and dependent care expenses. Attach Form 2441	**49**	
	50	Education credits from Form 8863, line 19	**50**	
	51	Retirement savings contributions credit. Attach Form 8880	**51**	
	52	Reserved	**52**	
	53	Residential energy credit. Attach Form 5695	**53**	
	54	Other credits from Form a ☐ 3800 b ☐ 8801 c ☐	**54**	
	55	Add the amounts in the far right column. Enter here and include on Form 1040, line 12	**55**	

For Paperwork Reduction Act Notice, see your tax return instructions.   Cat. No. 71480G   Schedule 3 (Form 1040) 2018

©2019 Internal Revenue Service

8

2018 Schedules 4, 5 & 6 - that support the 2018 Form 1040 postcard

SCHEDULE 4 (Form 1040)

Other Taxes

Department of the Treasury
Internal Revenue Service

▶ Attach to Form 1040.
▶ Go to *www.irs.gov/Form1040* for instructions and the latest information.

OMB No. 1545-0074

2018

Attachment Sequence No. 04

Name(s) shown on Form 1040 | Your social security number

Other Taxes

57	Self-employment tax. Attach Schedule SE	57	
58	Unreported social security and Medicare tax from: Form a ☐ 4137 b ☐ 8919	58	
59	Additional tax on IRAs, other qualified retirement plans, and other tax-favored accounts. Attach Form 5329 if required	59	
60a	Household employment taxes. Attach Schedule H	60a	
b	Repayment of first-time homebuyer credit from Form 5405. Attach Form 5405 if required	60b	
61	Health care: individual responsibility (see instructions)	61	
62	Taxes from: a ☐ Form 8959 b ☐ Form 8960 c ☐ Instructions; enter code(s) _____	62	
63	Section 965 net tax liability installment from Form 965-A 63		
64	Add the amounts in the far right column. These are your **total other taxes.** Enter here and on Form 1040, line 14	64	

For Paperwork Reduction Act Notice, see your tax return instructions.   Cat. No. 71481R   Schedule 4 (Form 1040) 2018

SCHEDULE 5 (Form 1040)

Other Payments and Refundable Credits

Department of the Treasury
Internal Revenue Service

▶ Attach to Form 1040.
▶ Go to *www.irs.gov/Form1040* for instructions and the latest information.

OMB No. 1545-0074

2018

Attachment Sequence No. 05

Name(s) shown on Form 1040 | Your social security number

Other Payments and Refundable Credits

65	Reserved	65	
66	2018 estimated tax payments and amount applied from 2017 return	66	
67a	Reserved	67a	
b	Reserved	67b	
68–69	Reserved	68–69	
70	Net premium tax credit. Attach Form 8962	70	
71	Amount paid with request for extension to file (see instructions)	71	
72	Excess social security and tier 1 RRTA tax withheld	72	
73	Credit for federal tax on fuels. Attach Form 4136	73	
74	Credits from Form: a ☐ 2439 b ☐ Reserved c ☐ 8885 d ☐ _____	74	
75	Add the amounts in the far right column. These are your total **other payments and refundable credits.** Enter here and include on Form 1040, line 17	75	

For Paperwork Reduction Act Notice, see your tax return instructions.   Cat. No. 71482C   Schedule 5 (Form 1040) 2018

SCHEDULE 6 (Form 1040)

Foreign Address and Third Party Designee

Department of the Treasury
Internal Revenue Service

▶ Attach to Form 1040.
▶ Go to *www.irs.gov/Form1040* for instructions and the latest information.

OMB No. 1545-0074

2018

Attachment Sequence No. 05A

Name(s) shown on Form 1040 | Your social security number

Foreign Address	Foreign country name	Foreign province/county	Foreign postal code
Third Party Designee	Do you want to allow another person to discuss this return with the IRS (see instructions)? ☐ **Yes.** Complete below. ☐ **No**		
	Designee's name ▶	Phone no. ▶	Personal identification number (PIN) ▶

For Paperwork Reduction Act Notice, see your tax return instructions.   Cat. No. 71483N   Schedule 6 (Form 1040) 2018

The President and Congress did not really "simplify" the Internal Revenue Code except for "suspending" the Personal Exemptions and doubling the Standard Deductions. They created new Code Sections that actually added complexity like the Qualified Business Income deduction. Congress "suspended" several deductions until 2026 that some taxpayers had benefited from, and modified other Credits that could increase refunds.

The President kept his promise that taxpayers could fill out their tax return on a "postcard" to be mailed in. That is why the IRS created the single-page 2018 Form 1040 postcard that can be folded and mailed in.

Very few taxpayers, though, will have such a simple tax scenario that can be completely described on the single-page 2018 Form 1040 postcard, without using one or more of the six new supporting Schedules.

A brief sampling of some of the major TCJA changes are listed below:
The Standard Deduction amounts have nearly doubled, as the Personal Exemptions have been eliminated from the 2018 Form 1040 postcard.

The Child Tax Credit has doubled to $2,000 and the income phase-out levels have been raised substantially to qualify many more Taxpayers.

There is now a $10,000/$5,000 per tax return limit on deducting State and Local Taxes, otherwise known as the SALT deduction.

Unless you are in the Military, a taxpayer can no longer deduct Qualified Moving Expenses related to relocating to a new city for a new job.

Taxpayers can no longer deduct Unreimbursed Business and/or Education Expenses related to their salary job. All other similar Miscellaneous Itemized Deductions formerly allowed above 2% of your Adjusted Gross Income (AGI) have been "suspended" until the 2026 tax year.

As a result of the Standard Deductions being nearly doubled far fewer Taxpayers will Itemize their Deductions. Therefore, they will no longer benefit from a deduction for Charitable Contributions. Charitable Contribution deductions are allowed only if you Itemize your Deductions.

Taxpayers can no longer deduct Casualty and Theft Losses as an Itemized Deduction category, unless they were incurred within a Federally Declared Disaster Area so specified by the President.

Software like TurboTax™ will be updated to reflect the new single-page 2018 Form 1040 postcard and its six new supporting Schedules.

Your Paid Preparer also will be trained to understand the new TCJA Tax Laws and forms, and his/her tax software will be updated accordingly.

Your final PDF or printed tax returns for the 2018 tax year will have an entirely new look, quite different from any recent tax years.

2) The revised 2018 Individual Income Tax Rate Brackets

The Tax Rates now reflect the slightly lower income tax rate brackets and the slightly increased income thresholds for each tax rate bracket. These affect the 2018 to 2025 tax years, adjusted yearly for inflation.

The Tax Policy Center gave these estimates of the 2018 tax savings:
- lowest-earning fifth - after-tax income* increased by 0.4 percent
- next-highest fifth - after-tax income increased by 1.2 percent
- next two quintiles - after-tax income increased by 1.6 percent and 1.9 percent respectively
- top-earning fifth - after-tax income increased by 2.9 percent
  * "after-tax income" means the income you can keep - after taxes

Tax Rate Schedules based on schedules in TheTaxBook™, redrawn by the Author for clarity.

2018 Federal Tax Rate Schedules

Single Filing Status - Taxable Income

$ 0 to	9,525	x 10.0%	minus	$ 0.00	= Tax
$ 9,526 to	38,700	x 12.0%	minus	$ 190.50	= Tax
$ 38,701 to	82,500	x 22.0%	minus	$ 4,060.50	= Tax
$ 82,501 to	157,500	x 24.0%	minus	$ 5,710.50	= Tax
$ 157,501 to	200,000	x 32.0%	minus	$ 18,310.50	= Tax
$ 200,001 to	500,000	x 35.0%	minus	$ 24,310.50	= Tax
$ 500,001 and	over	x 37.0%	minus	$ 34,310.50	= Tax

Married Filing Jointly|Qualifying Widow(er) Filing Status - Taxable Income

$ 0 to	19,050	x 10.0%	minus	$ 0.00	= Tax
$ 19,051 to	77,400	x 12.0%	minus	$ 381.00	= Tax
$ 77,401 to	165,000	x 22.0%	minus	$ 8,121.00	= Tax
$ 165,001 to	315,000	x 24.0%	minus	$ 11,421.00	= Tax
$ 315,001 to	400,000	x 32.0%	minus	$ 36,621.00	= Tax
$ 400,001 to	600,000	x 35.0%	minus	$ 48,621.00	= Tax
$ 600,001 and	over	x 37.0%	minus	$ 60,621.00	= Tax

Married Filing Separately Filing Status - Taxable Income

$ 0 to	9,525	x 10.0%	minus	$ 0.00	= Tax
$ 9,526 to	38,700	x 12.0%	minus	$ 190.50	= Tax
$ 38,701 to	82,500	x 22.0%	minus	$ 4,060.50	= Tax
$ 82,501 to	157,500	x 24.0%	minus	$ 5,710.50	= Tax
$ 157,501 to	200,000	x 32.0%	minus	$ 18,310.50	= Tax
$ 200,001 to	300,000	x 35.0%	minus	$ 24,310.50	= Tax
$ 300,001 and	over	x 37.0%	minus	$ 30,310.50	= Tax

Head of Household Filing Status - Taxable Income

$ 0 to	13,600	x 10.0%	minus	$ 0.00	= Tax
$ 13,601 to	51,800	x 12.0%	minus	$ 272.00	= Tax
$ 51,801 to	82,500	x 22.0%	minus	$ 5,452.00	= Tax
$ 82,501 to	157,500	x 24.0%	minus	$ 7,102.00	= Tax
$ 157,501 to	200,000	x 32.0%	minus	$ 19,702.00	= Tax
$ 200,001 to	500,000	x 35.0%	minus	$ 25,702.00	= Tax
$ 500,001 and	over	x 37.0%	minus	$ 35,702.00	= Tax

2017 Federal Tax Rate Schedules

Single Filing Status - Taxable Income

$ 0 to	9,325	x 10.0%	minus	$ 0.00	= Tax
$ 9,326 to	37,950	x 15.0%	minus	$ 466.25	= Tax
$ 37,951 to	91,900	x 25.0%	minus	$ 4,261.25	= Tax
$ 91,901 to	191,650	x 28.0%	minus	$ 7,018.25	= Tax
$ 191,651 to	416,700	x 33.0%	minus	$ 16,600.75	= Tax
$ 416,701 to	418,400	x 35.0%	minus	$ 24,934.75	= Tax
$ 418,401 and	over	x 39.6%	minus	$ 44,181.15	= Tax

Married Filing Jointly|Qualifying Widow(er) Filing Status - Taxable Income

$ 0 to	18,650	x 10.0%	minus	$ 0.00	= Tax
$ 18,651 to	75,900	x 15.0%	minus	$ 932.50	= Tax
$ 75,901 to	153,100	x 25.0%	minus	$ 8,522.50	= Tax
$ 153,101 to	233,350	x 28.0%	minus	$ 13,115.50	= Tax
$ 233,351 to	416,700	x 33.0%	minus	$ 24,783.00	= Tax
$ 416,701 to	470,700	x 35.0%	minus	$ 33,117.00	= Tax
$ 470,701 and	over	x 39.6%	minus	$ 54,769.20	= Tax

Married Filing Separately Filing Status - Taxable Income

$ 0 to	9,325	x 10.0%	minus	$ 0.00	= Tax
$ 9,326 to	37,950	x 15.0%	minus	$ 466.25	= Tax
$ 37,951 to	76,550	x 25.0%	minus	$ 4,261.25	= Tax
$ 76,551 to	116,675	x 28.0%	minus	$ 6,557.75	= Tax
$ 116,676 to	208,350	x 33.0%	minus	$ 12,391.50	= Tax
$ 208,351 to	235,350	x 35.0%	minus	$ 16,558.50	= Tax
$ 235,351 and	over	x 39.6%	minus	$ 27,384.60	= Tax

Head of Household Filing Status - Taxable Income

$ 0 to	13,350	x 10.0%	minus	$ 0.00	= Tax
$ 13,351 to	50,800	x 15.0%	minus	$ 667.50	= Tax
$ 50,801 to	131,200	x 25.0%	minus	$ 5,747.50	= Tax
$ 131,201 to	212,500	x 28.0%	minus	$ 9,683.50	= Tax
$ 212,501 to	416,700	x 33.0%	minus	$ 20,308.50	= Tax
$ 416,701 to	444,550	x 35.0%	minus	$ 26,642.50	= Tax
$ 444,551 and	over	x 39.6%	minus	$ 49,091.80	= Tax

See the graph table below that illustrates these after-tax income saving estimates and the Hyperlink to the article from the Tax Policy Center: https://www.taxpolicycenter.org/feature/analysis-tax-cuts-and-jobs-act

I included this chart as both sides of the political spectrum tend to disagree about who will benefit, and who will not benefit, from the TCJA changes to the 2018 Individual Income Tax Rate Brackets.

FIGURE 1

Percent Change in After-tax Income of the Conference Agreement for the Tax Cuts and Jobs Act
By expanded cash income percentile, 2018, 2025, and 2027

TPC

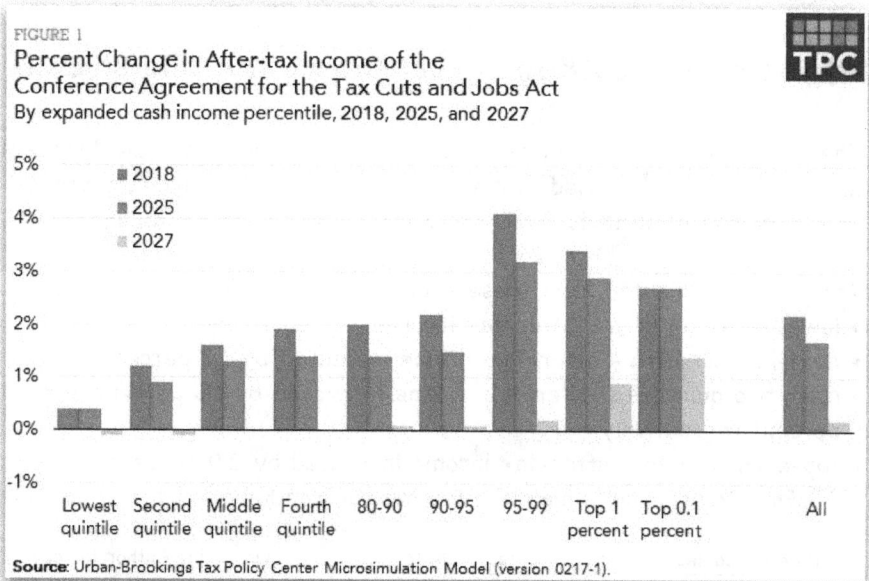

Legend: ■ 2018 ■ 2025 ■ 2027

X-axis categories: Lowest quintile, Second quintile, Middle quintile, Fourth quintile, 80-90, 90-95, 95-99, Top 1 percent, Top 0.1 percent, All

Y-axis: -1% to 5%

Source: Urban-Brookings Tax Policy Center Microsimulation Model (version 0217-1).

As an IRS Enrolled Agent, part of my job is to provide Taxpayers and my Clients the information they need to make informed decisions about their tax scenario. I always remain politically neutral and attempt to only describe the realized cause and effect of any new tax legislation.

Taxpayers will have seen first-hand by April 15th, 2019 if these TCJA major tax law changes have increased or decreased their 2018 refunds.

One issue that arose from the recent 2018 tax year, is that many Taxpayers received smaller refunds than they had anticipated. This was due in large part to the new payroll withholding tables introduced in early 2018 by the IRS, to reflect the lower 2018 tax rates. Taxpayers then began receiving more take-home pay in each paycheck. Conversely, less tax was being taken out of each paycheck, so less "tax savings" accrued throughout the rest of the year. The tax obligation for many taxpayers went down in 2018, but these withholding changes altered many refunds.

3) The revised 2018 Capital Gain Tax Rate Schedule

The Capital Gain Tax Rate Schedule is calculated differently in 2018 and beyond, as it is no longer based on the Income Tax Rate Brackets. The Capital Gain Tax Rates are now based on your Filing Status and Taxable Income level, for the 2018 to 2025 tax years, adjusted for inflation.

For Example:
- A Single taxpayer would pay no tax on his or her Capital Gain income if their Taxable Income level was between $0 to $38,600.
- They would pay a maximum 15% Capital Gain Tax Rate if their Taxable Income was in the range between $38,601 to $425,800.

Typically Capital Gain income subject to the lower Capital Gain Tax Rates comes from selling mutual fund shares or stocks that were held for more than one year. These are considered a Long-Term Capital Gain. Your broker will identify these sales on your year-end 1099-B forms.

Qualified Stock Dividends and long-term Capital Gain Distributions are also subject to and benefit from the lower Capital Gain Tax Rates. Your Broker will identify these as shown on your year-end 1099-DIV form.

Capital Gain Tax Rate Schedule based on the schedule in TheTaxBook™, redrawn by the Author for clarity.

2018 Capital Gain Tax Rate Schedule

Single Filing Status - Taxable Income

$	0	to	38,600	maximum rate =	0%
$	38,601	to	425,800	maximum rate =	15%
$	425,801	and	over	maximum rate =	20%

Married Filing Jointly|Qualifying Widow(er) Filing Status - Taxable Income

$	0	to	77,200	maximum rate =	0%
$	77,201	to	479,000	maximum rate =	15%
$	479,001	and	over	maximum rate =	20%

Married Filing Separately Filing Status - Taxable Income

$	0	to	38,600	maximum rate =	0%
$	38,601	to	239,500	maximum rate =	15%
$	239,501	and	over	maximum rate =	20%

Head of Household Filing Status - Taxable Income

$	0	to	51,700	maximum rate =	0%
$	51,701	to	452,400	maximum rate =	15%
$	452,401	and	over	maximum rate =	20%

Estates & Trusts - Taxable Income

$	0	to	2,600	maximum rate =	0%
$	2,601	to	12,700	maximum rate =	15%
$	12,701	and	over	maximum rate =	20%

Chapter 2:

Personal Exemptions and Dependent Credits

TOPICS SUMMARY #4 to #6

4) The Personal Exemption deduction amounts have been removed from the 2018 Form 1040 postcard

The Personal Exemption deduction amounts previously listed on the tax return for the Taxpayer, the Spouse, any Qualifying Child and any Qualifying Relative - have been removed from the 2018 Form 1040 postcard. This is in effect for tax years 2018 through 2025.

The TCJA legislation set the Personal Exemption amount to be Zero after December 31st, 2017, and before January 1st, 2026.

5) The Child Tax Credit has doubled to $2,000 with $1,400 now refundable as the Additional Child Tax Credit component

The Child Tax Credit has doubled to $2,000 per eligible Qualifying Child under the age of 17, up from the previous $1,000. The refundable component of the Child Tax Credit – called the Additional Child Tax Credit – has increased to $1,400 from the previous $1,000.

The income levels under which a taxpayer may claim the Child Tax Credit have increased substantially, such that many more taxpayers will benefit from the credit.

Income levels up to $400,000 (MAGI) for a Married Filing Jointly couple and up to $200,000 (MAGI) for all other Filing Statuses.

6) A new nonrefundable $500 Credit for Other Dependents added

A new nonrefundable $500 Credit for Other Dependents is available for any Qualifying Child and/or Qualifying Relative listed on your tax return - who would not be eligible for the Child Tax Credit.

4) The Personal Exemption deduction amounts have been removed from the 2018 Form 1040 postcard

The Personal Exemption deduction amount for the Taxpayer, the Spouse, any Qualifying Child and any Qualifying Relative – has been set to Zero after December 31st, 2017 and before January 1st, 2026. Therefore Personal Exemptions have been removed from the 2018 Form 1040 postcard.

All the rules for the previous Personal Exemption deduction amount remain in the Internal Revenue Code (IRC) ready to be reactivated if and when the Congress would reinstate the Personal Exemption amount to be above Zero. See this Internal Revenue Code Section at:

https://www.law.cornell.edu/uscode/text/26/151

The Law School at Cornell University manages this Internal Revenue Code web site. It is a favorite web site for myself, a true "Tax Geek", who reads and studies the actual text of the Internal Revenue Code (IRC). A Google search per Code Section description works very well to then display the Internal Revenue Code section being researched.

For example:
Type into Google " IRC Personal Exemption " and the first Hyperlink listed will be from this Cornell Law School web site. The link will read:

26 U.S. Code §151. Allowance of deductions for personal exemptions

Prior to the passage of the TCJA legislation, the Personal Exemption deduction amount had been determined by the IRS to be $4,150 per person listed on your tax return for the 2018 tax year. This deduction would have been $4,150 each for the Taxpayer, Spouse, each Qualifying Child and each Qualifying Relative on the 2018 return. The TCJA legislation instead, set the Personal Exemption deduction amount to be Zero.

The now higher $2,000 Child Tax Credit and the new $500 Credit for Other Dependents – were designed by Congress to somewhat compensate for the elimination of the Personal Exemption deduction amount.

The doubling of the Standard Deduction was also designed to help mitigate the loss of this Personal Exemption deduction amount.

5) The Child Tax Credit has doubled to $2,000 with $1,400 now refundable as the Additional Child Tax Credit

The Child Tax Credit has doubled to $2,000 per eligible Qualifying Child listed on your tax return, with the refundable Additional Child Tax Credit component increased to $1,400 per eligible Qualifying Child.

The credit is available for each Qualifying Child under age 17 on December 31st, listed on your tax return, with a valid Social Security Number.

In recent tax years a Qualifying Child under age 17 with an ITIN number (Individual Taxpayer Identification Number) would also be eligible for the Child Tax Credit. For the 2018 through to the 2025 tax years, each eligible Qualifying Child must have a Social Security Number, valid for work, to qualify the taxpayer for the Child Tax Credit.

The Child Tax Credit can only reduce your Form 1040 postcard, line 11 Initial Tax Obligation down to zero, but not below zero. It is considered a nonrefundable credit. Nonrefundable credits can only be used to reduce the line 11 Initial Tax Obligation down to zero.

The Additional Child Tax Credit component can actually add to your refund even if your line 11 Initial Tax Obligation has been reduced down to zero. It is a refundable credit based on the amount of your yearly Earned Income. Each Qualifying Child must have a Social Security Number to qualify for the refundable Additional Child Tax Credit component.

The Earned Income threshold has decreased to $2,500 from the previous $3,000. This is used to calculate how much of that refundable $1,400 per child Additional Child Tax Credit component you will qualify for. It calculates as 15% of your Earned Income over this $2,500 threshold up to the $1,400 allowed per each Qualifying Child you have listed on your tax return, that also qualifies for the Child Tax Credit.
For Example:
A taxpayer with Earned Income of $11,833 or more is potentially eligible for the full $1,400 for one child's Additional Child Tax Credit component.
• ($11,833 minus $2,500 = $9,333) so ($9,333 times 15% = $1,400) •

The Child Tax Credit and the Additional Child Tax Credit component work together for a maximum credit of $2,000 per eligible Qualifying Child.

<u>For Example</u>: Consider this scenario for the 2018 Child Tax Credit:

Your son age 9 and daughter age 11 each are listed as a Qualifying Child on your tax return. They are both under the age of 17 on December 31st, 2018 and each possess a valid Social Security Number. That would then potentially qualify you for the $2,000 each for your son and daughter for the Child Tax Credit for a total of $4,000. That $4,000 could then be used to reduce your Initial Tax Obligation down to zero.

Now let's assume your Initial Tax Obligation, line 11 of the new Form 1040 postcard, after the Standard Deduction is only $1,700. That means you could only use $1,700 of your up to "maximum $4,000 Child Tax Credit" to reduce this line 11 Initial Tax Obligation down to zero.

That would leave $2,300 of unused Child Tax Credits that you could possibly use — as a refund — if your Earned Income level qualifies you for the Additional Child Tax Credit component. Earned Income is for personal services like a salary job. It does not include investment income.

The Additional Child Tax Credit component then calculates if your Earned Income was high enough to qualify you to benefit from this full $2,300 of your unused Child Tax Credits to be applied as a tax refund. You can use up to $1,400 of unused Child Tax Credits per Qualifying Child for the Additional Child Tax Credit component, up to $2,300 in this example.

The amount of your Earned Income above $2,500 is multiplied by 15%, to determine how much of that Additional Child Tax Credit you can use.

If the Earned Income value in this example was at least $17,833, then you would benefit from the $2,300 of these unused Child Tax Credits.
• $17,833 minus $2,500 equals $15,333
• $15,333 times 15% equals $2,300

You would then qualify to use the full $2,300 of your refundable Additional Child Tax Credit component. Your tax refund would then be increased by this $2,300 value, or your other tax owed will be decreased by the same $2,300 amount - like to reduce your self-employment tax.

The income phase-out levels have increased substantially for the 2018 tax year such that many more families with children will qualify to receive the Child Tax Credit. See the next page for these income levels.

The Child Tax Credit begins to phase-out when the Married Filing Jointly couple's 2018 Modified Adjusted Gross Income (MAGI) exceeds $400,000. In recent tax years that phase-out level started at $110,000 for the Married Filing Jointly (MFJ) couple.

The Child Tax Credit will begin to phase-out by $50 for each $1,000 the MFJ 2018 income exceeds $400,000. Therefore the credit would not be allowed for MFJ incomes above the $440,000 level for one child. An additional $40,000 of income phase-out is used for each additional child.

The Child Tax Credit begins to phase-out for all other taxpayer Filing Statuses when their 2018 Modified Adjusted Gross Income (MAGI) exceeds $200,000. In recent tax years that phase-out level was $75,000 for the Single, the Head of Household and the Qualifying Widow(er) filing statuses and $55,000 for the Married Filing Separately filing status.

The Child Tax Credit begins to phase-out by $50 for each $1,000 these other Taxpayer's 2018 income exceeds $200,000. The credit would not be allowed for incomes above the $240,000 level for one child. An additional $40,000 of income phase-out is used for each additional child.

These new Child Tax Credit and Additional Child Tax Credit TCJA tax law changes are in effect for the tax years 2018 through to 2025.

Of course the tax software automatically calculates this for you.

Refer to the links below for the IRS forms that perform all the Child Tax Credit calculations. Sometimes it is informative to print out the actual IRS tax forms that calculate a Credit. You then can follow the logic of how your tax information qualifies you for the Child Tax Credit.

2018 Child Tax Credit and Credit for Other Dependents worksheet
on pages 42 to 43 of the Form 1040 instructions in the PDF below
https://www.irs.gov/pub/irs-pdf/i1040gi.pdf

Schedule 8812_Additional Child Tax Credit
https://www.irs.gov/pub/irs-pdf/f1040s8.pdf

Schedule 8812_Instructions
https://www.irs.gov/pub/irs-pdf/i1040s8.pdf

6) A new nonrefundable $500
Credit for Other Dependents added

A new $500 nonrefundable Credit for Other Dependents is now available for any Dependent listed on your tax return that is not an eligible Qualifying Child for the Child Tax Credit. A Dependent is defined as a Qualifying Child or Qualifying Relative that satisfies the IRS eligibility requirements to be listed on your tax return as a Dependent. This new credit is in effect for the 2018 through to the 2025 tax years.

If your Qualifying Child is age 17 or older on December 31st, they will not be eligible for the Child Tax Credit. They would instead qualify you for this Credit for Other Dependents. This requirement also applies to any Child who is "permanently and totally disabled" and age 17 or older on December 31st. They are not eligible for the Child Tax Credit.

The Gross Income Test for a Qualifying Relative is $4,150 for the 2018 tax year. This means for a person to be listed on your tax return as your Qualifying Relative, they cannot have taxable Gross Income at or above this $4,150 threshold. They can have non-taxable income such as Tax-Exempt Interest or Social Security not included in the $4,150 total.

This $4,150 Gross Income Test does not apply to a Qualifying Child. If your Qualifying Child earns money, they can still be listed as your Dependent providing they did not use the money they earned to pay for more than half of their own support living in your household. They can still use the money they earned for savings or personal expenses.

This $500 Credit for Other Dependents can help reduce your line 11 Initial Tax Obligation to zero, but not below zero. It is not a refundable credit like the $1,400 per child Additional Child Tax Credit component.

A Qualifying Child and/or Qualifying Relative who does not possess a valid Social Security Number can still qualify you for this Credit for Other Dependents. They can apply for an ITIN number (Individual Taxpayer Identification Number) to qualify as a Dependent for this credit.

The 2018 income phase-out levels for this Credit for Other Dependents are the same as for the Child Tax Credit. Those being $400,000 (MAGI) for the MFJ couple and $200,000 (MAGI) for all other taxpayers.

Chapter 3:

Standard Deduction and Itemized Deductions changes

TOPICS SUMMARY #7 to #19

7) The 2018 Standard Deduction amounts have almost doubled to:

$12,000 for the **Single** and **Married Filing Separately** filing status

$18,000 for the **Head of Household** filing status

$24,000 for the **Married Filing Jointly** filing status

$24,000 for the **Qualifying Widow(er)** filing status

8) The phase-out of Itemized Deductions "suspended" for higher-incomes

In the 2017 tax year certain Itemized Deductions could be reduced by up to 80% if your Adjusted Gross Income was above these levels:
- Single - $261,500
- Married Filing Jointly or Qualifying Widow(er) - $313,800
- Married Filing Separately - $156,900
- Head of Household - $287,650

This phase-out limitation has been "suspended" until 01/01/2026

9) Far fewer taxpayers will now benefit from the Itemized Deductions

Meaning the taxpayer would get a larger deduction from their Adjusted Gross Income (AGI) using the now higher Standard Deduction, as compared to any Itemized Deductions total they could use.

10) The Miscellaneous Itemized Deductions subject to the 2% of Adjusted Gross Income (AGI) threshold are "suspended"

Many previously allowed Itemized Deductions such as Unreimbursed Business and/or Education Expenses for your salary job - are "suspended" until 01/01/2026. These were previously allowed if they totaled above 2% of your Adjusted Gross Income for the tax year.

11) The 7.5% AGI threshold for 2018 Medical Expenses deduction retained

It remains at 7.5% for 2018 but rises back up to 10% for the 2019 tax year and beyond. These are unreimbursed Medical Expenses you list as an Itemized Deduction on the Schedule A. You can deduct 2018 Medical Expenses above this 7.5% AGI income threshold.

12) The new $10,000/$5,000 per tax return limit for the SALT deductions

SALT stands for the State and Local Tax deduction. This is the aggregate total of taxes paid for Real Estate Tax on your home(s), the State Income Tax or State Sales Tax you paid, and the State Personal Property Tax you paid. In previous tax years there was no limit on the amount of this aggregated SALT deduction.

13) The lower Mortgage Interest Deduction limits for new mortgages
   • For new mortgages secured after 12/15/2017, the mortgage limit is:
   • $375,000 Mortgage total limit for Married Filing Separately
   • $750,000 Mortgage total limit for all other Filing Statuses

14) The deduction for Interest on Home Equity Loans is now limited

The Home Equity Loan must have been used to buy, build or substantially improve the taxpayer's home that secures the loan.

15) Mortgage Insurance Premiums are no longer an Itemized Deduction

Previously they were listed along with your Mortgage Interest. This was not included in the TCJA legislation to extend this deduction.

16) Fewer Taxpayers will qualify to deduct their Charitable Contributions

Your Itemized Deductions total has to be more than the new higher Standard Deduction to benefit from a Charitable Contribution. Charitable Contributions are listed as an Itemized Deduction category.

Your Charitable Contributions added to all of your other Itemized Deduction categories, must total to be more than the Standard Deduction. You typically deduct the higher of these two values.

17) Charitable Contributions - two rule changes

You can now deduct cash Charitable Contributions you make to public charities and certain private foundations, up to 60% of your Adjusted Gross Income (AGI). Previously that limit was 50% of AGI.

You are no longer allowed to deduct 80% of the alumni contribution you made to your alma mater college to gain access to purchase season tickets for athletic events - like for college football games. This contribution gave you the right to purchase such tickets, often referred to as a seat-license fee.

18) Non-disaster Casualty and Theft losses no longer deductible

Only Casualty and Theft losses incurred in a Federally Declared Disaster Area will be deductible as an Itemized Deduction category in the 2018 tax year through to the 2025 tax year. Other similar losses not in a Disaster Area are no longer normally deductible, unless used to offset personal casualty gains that you might have received from insurance reimbursements.

19) The Living Expense deduction for Members of Congress eliminated

They previously were allowed to deduct $3,000 as a Miscellaneous Itemized Deduction to reimburse themselves for Living Expenses they incurred for their time serving in Washington, D.C. during the work week while away from their home State and District.

7) The 2018 Standard Deduction amounts have almost doubled

The 2018 tax year Standard Deduction amounts have almost doubled to:

$12,000 for the **Single, Married Filing Separately (MFS)** filing status
- add $1,600 if age 65 or older for Single, add $1,300 for (MFS)
- add $1,600 if blind for Single, add $1,300 for (MFS)

$18,000 for the **Head of Household** filing status
- add $1,600 if age 65 or older
- add $1,600 if blind

$24,000 for **Married Filing Jointly, Qualifying Widow(er)** filing status
- add $1,300 for each spouse or qualifying widow(er) age 65 or older
- add $1,300 for each blind spouse or blind qualifying widow(er)

If you are age 65 or older on December 31st of the tax year, blind, or both - you add these additional amounts to your Standard Deduction.

For Example: You use the Single filing status and you are age 68
- $12,000 regular Standard Deduction for the Single filing status
- $1,600 additional Standard Deduction for being age 65 or older
- $13,600 total Standard Deduction ($12,000 + $1,600 = $13,600)

The Standard Deduction values will then be increased yearly by being adjusted for inflation for the succeeding tax years 2019 through 2025.

8) The phase-out of the Itemized Deductions has been "suspended" for higher-income Taxpayers

In recent tax years certain Itemized Deductions were phased-out for higher-income Taxpayers. This has been "suspended" until 01/01/2026.

For Example: a Single person with an Adjusted Gross Income (AGI) over $261,500 in 2017, would have had certain Itemized Deductions begun to be phased-out, by up to 80% of these Itemized Deductions. Refer back to item #8 in the TOPICS SUMMARY, page 21 for the phase-out levels.

9) Far fewer taxpayers will now benefit from the Itemized Deductions

Fewer Taxpayers will Itemize their Deductions on their 2018 tax returns as the new nearly doubled 2018 Standard Deduction amounts will be a better value for many Taxpayers. In the previous 2016 tax year around 30% of Taxpayers benefited by using their higher Itemized Deductions total, according to the IRS figures. With the new TCJA tax law changes, it is now estimated that only 10% of Taxpayers will Itemize their Deductions in the 2018 tax year, according to the Tax Policy Center.
See this article describing these statistics.
https://www.taxpolicycenter.org/briefing-book/what-are-itemized-deductions-and-who-claims-them

Fewer taxpayers will Itemized their Deductions on their 2018 tax return – in part because of these several TCJA tax law changes listed below:
- The SALT (State and Local Taxes) deduction is now limited to $10,000 per tax return and $5,000 for a Married Filing Separately taxpayer.
- The total deduction for Mortgage Interest and Home Equity Loan Interest has decreased for new loans secured after 12-15-2017.
- With the near doubling of the Standard Deductions, fewer people will be able to take the deduction for their Charitable Contributions – as their total Itemized Deductions will not be more than the new higher Standard Deduction value. Charitable Contributions can only be listed as an Itemized Deduction category.
- Personal Casualty and Theft Losses are no longer deductible as an Itemized Deduction, unless the casualty or theft event happened in a Federally Declared Disaster Area, as designated by the President.
- The Miscellaneous Itemized Deductions subject to the 2% of Adjusted Gross Income threshold have been "suspended" until 01/01/2026.
  - This included unreimbursed job expenses and job-related education expenses you incurred for your regular salary job.
  - This included any home office expenses you needed to incur for your remote salary job if your wages were reported to you on a normal W-2 form from your employer.
  - This included client-related travel and meal expenses you incurred to service your sales clients, as a non-statutory salaried salesperson, if your wages were reported to you on a normal W-2 form.
  - Taxpayers can also no longer deduct the other categories of Miscellaneous Deductions also subject to the 2% of AGI threshold.

10) The Miscellaneous Itemized Deductions subject to the 2% of AGI threshold are "suspended" until 01/01/2026

Miscellaneous Itemized Deductions related to your job/work and other personal expenses listed below, formerly allowed in total as a deduction above 2% of your Adjusted Gross Income (AGI), have been eliminated from the 2018 Schedule A form that lists Itemized Deduction categories. They are suspended until 01/01/2026.

- work-related travel, transportation, and vehicle mileage
  - Including Department Of Transportation (DOT) per diems
- work-related meals, gifts and lodging
- union dues
- business liability insurance premiums
- depreciation on a computer/cellular telephone your employer required you to use for your work or for personal investments you managed
- memberships in and dues to professional societies
- work-related education to improve your current job skills
- home office expenses for that part of your home you used regularly and exclusively for your remote salary job work
- expenses of looking for a new job in your present occupation
- legal fees related to the income you earned at your job
- professional licenses and regulatory fees related to your job
  - such as for Lawyers, Doctors, Architects, etc.
- malpractice, errors & omissions, etc. insurance for your salary job
- subscriptions to professional journals and trade magazines related to your work, such as Medical Journals or Architectural Design magazines
- tools and supplies used in your work
- work clothes and uniforms for your job
  - if required and not suitable for everyday use, like a Nurse's uniform
- educator expenses in excess of $250
- investment advisory and management fees for your investments
- fees for legal and tax advice related to your investments
- appraisal fees for casualty losses and/or charitable donations
- trustee fees to manage IRAs and other investment accounts
- rental fees for a bank safe deposit box
  - to safely keep your investment paperwork, stock certificates, etc.
- tax preparation and tax advice fees
- hobby expenses used to offset your hobby income
- fees to contest the IRS for any audit, collection or refund matter
- certain personal legal fees, like to recover alimony from a spouse

- If you were a salaried employee, and worked from a home office "For the Convenience of your Employer", you will no longer be able to deduct the expenses related to that home office.
- If you were a non-statutory salaried salesperson, you will no longer be able to deduct the cost of your travel to/from sales calls, or the client meal expenses you incurred for your sales clients.

Many companies will now have to implement Accountable Reimbursement Plans to reimburse these typical expenses incurred by such salaried employees, who in recent tax years could deduct these unreimbursed job expenses on their tax returns, as a Miscellaneous Itemized Deduction expense subject to the 2% of AGI threshold. The employee will now have to submit the expense receipts for the company reimbursement.
Per the IRS: To be an Accountable Plan, your employer's reimbursement or allowance arrangement must include all three of the following rules:
- You must have paid or incurred expenses that are deductible to the business while performing services as an employee
- You must adequately account to your employer for these expenses within a reasonable time period, and
- You must return any excess reimbursement or allowance within a reasonable time period

If you are a business owner or self-employed consultant, you can still deduct many of these categories of Miscellaneous expenses. You deduct these expense categories on the Schedule C (Form 1040) that reports your business income and expenses on your Individual tax return.

New York, California and some other States still allow these "subject to the 2% threshold" Misc. Deductions on their State income tax returns.

11) The 7.5% AGI threshold for deducting Medical Expenses as an Itemized Deduction remains for 2018

The threshold will revert back up to 10% of your AGI with the 2019 tax year and beyond. For 2018 tax returns, you can deduct the amount of your out-of-pocket, unreimbursed medical expenses that are above 7.5% of your Adjusted Gross Income (AGI). Calculate this on the Schedule A.
For Example: Your AGI is $65,000, so (7.5% of $65,000) is $4,875. Medical expenses above this 7.5% threshold of $4,875 would be deductible.
See the Schedule A at: https://www.irs.gov/pub/irs-pdf/f1040sa.pdf

12) The new $10,000/$5,000 per tax return limit for the SALT deductions

There is a $10,000 ($5,000 for Married Filing Separately) per tax return limit on deducting as Itemized Deduction categories the total of:
• State and Local Property Taxes you paid
• State and Local Income Taxes or State and Local Sales Taxes you paid
• State and Local Personal Property Taxes you paid
Otherwise known as the SALT deduction (State and Local Taxes)

Beginning with the first federal income tax in 1861 up through the 2017 tax year, there was always a deduction for all of, or a significant portion of, the SALT taxes paid in each tax year. This deduction is recorded on the Schedule A in the section called "Taxes You Paid". This limitation on the SALT deduction is in effect until the end of the 2025 tax year.

This could reduce the normally higher SALT deduction for many higher-income individuals living in States with both Income and Property Taxes. Four of those States have sued the IRS to have this provision repealed. See the lawsuit link below:
http://d31hzlhk6di2h5.cloudfront.net/20180717/23/db/ed/79/0c0cd-f707c0fe2fcea172831/SALT_COMPLAINT.pdf

Since these State's residents will only be able to deduct $10,000 of State Income and Property Taxes, the lawsuit claims the new SALT limitation unfairly raises the Federal Tax burden for their State's residents.

Conversely States with no Income Tax like Texas, Florida, etc. have asserted they were subsidizing these higher-taxed States, as their high-income residents paid more Federal tax on the same amount of income.

This is a very contentious political tax issue that will ultimately and most probably be decided by the U.S. Supreme Court.

Prepaid 2018 tax year property taxes would have been deductible in the 2017 tax year, only if they were assessed by your State or Local Government in late 2017, and you paid those 2018 assessed taxes in 2017.

The deduction for your foreign property taxes paid, not related to a rental income property, is no longer allowed for 2018 to 2025 tax years.

13) The new lower Mortgage Interest Deduction limits for new home mortgages secured after 12-15-2017

There is a lower Mortgage Interest Deduction limit on total mortgage home acquisition debt values, for new primary and secondary homes, for mortgage applications begun after December 15th, 2017. These new limitations are in effect for the 2018 to the 2025 tax years.
- Total Mortgages with a value up to $750,000 versus the previous $1,000,000 for all filing statuses except Married Filing Separately.
- Total Mortgages with a value up to $375,000 versus the previous $500,000 for a Married Filing Separately taxpayer.

The previous $1,000,000 limit still applies to mortgages closed on the purchase of a primary residence before January 1st, 2018, and those who then purchased that primary residence before April 1st, 2018.
- Providing the above described new mortgage application process had begun before December 15th, 2017 and entered into with a written binding contract.

The previous $1,000,000 limit also applies to the total of any older mortgages secured on or before December 15th, 2017. There are many circumstances that can affect your total mortgage size, so consult your mortgage lender for your 2018 tax year Form 1098 Mortgage Interest Statement. The bank will advise you what is considered mortgage home acquisition debt versus mortgage home equity acquisition debt. These mortgage size limits then determine how much mortgage interest you can deduct each year. If the remaining mortgage values are over the above described limits, you pro-rate down the interest you can deduct.

For Example, consider this simple scenario to illustrate this limitation:
Suppose you had in 2018 outstanding (pre December 16th, 2017) average original mortgage home acquisition debt balances of $1,200,000 on your primary residence and vacation home and you paid $42,000 in total mortgage interest.
- The (pre December 16th, 2017) combined mortgage home acquisition debt limit is $1,000,000. So you are $200,000 over the limit.
- Your pro-rated mortgage home acquisition debt percentage limit is calculated:
  - ($1,000,000) divided by ($1,200,000) equals 83.3%, to three decimal places.
  - ($42,000 in original mortgage interest) times the (0.833% pro-rated mortgage home acquisition debt percentage limit) equals $34,986
- Therefore your allowed mortgage interest deduction on this combined mortgage home acquisition debt would be lowered to $34,986 on your 2018 tax year return. This being pro-rated down from the original $42,000 interest value, as your total combined mortgage home acquisition debt exceeded the $1,000,000 (pre December 16th, 2017) limit by the $200,000.

14) The deduction for Interest on Home Equity Loans is now limited

Interest paid on a Home Equity Loan is no longer deductible, unless it was used to buy, build or substantially improve the taxpayer's home that secures the loan. See IRS Pub. 936-Home Mortgage Interest Deduction, in the What's New on page 1. https://www.irs.gov/publications/p936

Previously interest paid on up to $100,000 of a home equity loan was deductible even if you used the proceeds for other expenses not related to improving your primary residence — like paying personal bills, funds for a child's college tuition, or money to purchase that sailboat used at your vacation home. That added up to a combined limit of $1,100,000 for mortgages and the home equity loan. The deduction limit was $50,000 for a home equity loan value for a Married Filing Separately taxpayer.

Now the proceeds from the home equity loan must be and/or have been used to buy, build or substantially improve your home — to report the interest you paid on the home equity loan as an Itemized Deduction category on your 2018 tax return. The IRS has stated in the Publication 936: "The Home Equity Loan must have been used to buy, build or substantially improve the taxpayer's home that secures the loan."

This includes older home equity loans taken out before the new TCJA legislation. If the proceeds of that older home equity loan were not used to buy, build or substantially improve your home that secures the loan, the interest you paid in 2018 on that older home equity loan will no longer be deductible as an Itemized Deduction on the Schedule A form. It must be considered mortgage home equity acquisition debt.
- Your total new mortgage and new home equity debt cannot exceed the $750,000 limit, if the loans were secured after December 15th, 2017.
- The previous $1,100,000 combined limit also has been lowered to $1,000,000 for any older mortgages plus home equity loans secured on or before December 15th, 2017, considered as acquisition indebtedness.
- The older home equity loan, again, must have been used directly for that home which secures the loan, to deduct the interest paid in 2018.
- These new changes affect the 2018 through to the 2025 tax years.
See this article from the IRS which clears up much of the confusion: https://www.irs.gov/newsroom/interest-on-home-equity-loans-often-still-deductible-under-new-law

15) Mortgage Insurance Premiums are no longer deductible as an Itemized Deduction category

Mortgage Insurance Premiums are no longer deductible as an Itemized Deduction category on the 2018 tax year Schedule A. In previous tax years they were listed along with the Mortgage Interest deduction. The deduction for Mortgage Insurance Premiums was not extended by Congress past the 2017 tax year, and not included in the TCJA legislation.

Lenders typically require Mortgage Insurance until the FHA-backed mortgage debt is reduced to 78% of the home's value – for a 15-yr mortgage. A homeowner with a 30-yr FHA-backed mortgage typically also has to make 5-years of mortgage payments before the bank will remove the requirement to have mortgage insurance. You can typically refinance to a conventional loan after that 78% threshold, to then no longer have the FHA requirements to carry the mortgage insurance.

16) Fewer Taxpayers will now qualify to deduct their Charitable Contributions

As a result of the Standard Deduction values being almost doubled, fewer Taxpayers will Itemize their Deductions. Therefore, these taxpayers will no longer benefit from a deduction for Charitable Contributions. A tax benefit for Charitable Contributions is allowed only if you Itemize your Deductions. You deduct Charitable Contributions on the Schedule A.

Taxpayers can of course still donate to their favorite charities, but may not get a tax benefit unless they qualify to claim the Itemized Deductions. Some Taxpayers are now planning to "pool" their donations to report every two years, to then have their total Charitable Contribution amounts be large enough, every two years, to enable them to qualify for that Itemized Deduction benefit for charitable giving.

"These changes will shrink the number of households claiming an itemized deduction category for their gifts to charities from about 37 million down to about 16 million in the 2018 tax year."[2] "This will reduce the federal income tax subsidy for charitable giving by one-third, from about $63 billion down to roughly $42 billion."[2] [2] https://www.taxpolicy-center.org/briefing-book/how-did-tcja-affect-incentives-charitable-giving

17) Charitable Contributions - two rule changes

You can now deduct cash Charitable Contributions you make to public charities and certain private foundations, up to 60% of your Adjusted Gross Income (AGI). It had been limited to 50% of your AGI in recent tax years. This change is in effect for the tax years 2018 to 2025.

You can no longer deduct the alumni contribution you make to your alma mater college, to gain the right to purchase season tickets to athletic events like college football games. In recent tax years, you were allowed to deduct up to 80% of the cost you paid for such a seat-license fee.

18) Non-disaster Casualty and Theft losses are no longer deductible as an Itemized Deduction category

Taxpayers can no longer deduct Casualty and Theft Losses as an Itemized Deduction category unless incurred within a Federally Declared Disaster Area where the Casualty and Theft events happened. Non-disaster, personal casualty losses as a deduction have been "suspended" until January 1st, 2026.

Per Example:
- If a tree falls on your house, if you total your car in an accident, or your diamond ring is stolen...
- You can no longer claim those personal casualties, accidents, or thefts as an Itemized Deduction category unless they happened as a cause from and within a Federally Declared Disaster Area.

If you receive insurance reimbursements for non-disaster personal casualty or theft losses, that will create a taxable casualty gain, you can offset those taxable reimbursements with the actual personal casualty or theft losses. This will help to reduce the amount of the insurance reimbursements that could qualify as a taxable casualty gain.

Taxpayers with personal casualty losses not attributable to a federally declared disaster, may deduct those losses to the extent of personal casualty gains, per the Internal Revenue Code Section §165(h)(5)(B).
Per the IRS Publication 547 in the "What's New" on the front page:
"You will reduce your personal casualty gains by any casualty losses not attributable to a federally declared disaster."

19) The Living Expense deduction for Members of Congress eliminated

The Miscellaneous Itemized Deduction for Living Expenses for the Members of Congress while away from their home has been eliminated.

Members of Congress previously could deduct up to $3,000 of yearly Living Expenses, as a Miscellaneous Itemized Deduction, for their accommodations while serving on the behalf of their constituents during their work week in Washington, D.C. while away from their home State.

Since normal Taxpayers are no longer able to deduct the Miscellaneous Itemized Deductions subject to the 2% of AGI threshold, it was thought Members of Congress should no longer benefit from this deduction.

U.S. Senator Joni Ernst (R-Iowa) had this to say about this deduction:

"To achieve the ultimate goal of lowering tax rates for hardworking families and businesses, Congress is going to have to eliminate various loopholes and deductions in our outdated tax code. Congress should lead by example and offer up its own unnecessary tax break".

Congress did just that, and this $3,000 congressional tax break is gone.

See the link below to Senator Ernst's press release regarding this issue.
https://www.ernst.senate.gov/public/index.cfm/press-releases?ID=2062475B-0CAE-4558-B93A-CD9C10D25457

Chapter 4:

Income Adjustments and Deduction Changes

TOPICS SUMMARY #20 to #27

20) <u>Qualified Moving Expenses are no longer deductible for most taxpayers</u>

Unless you are an active duty Military Personnel and were ordered to move to a new duty station. The exclusion for company provided moving expense reimbursements also has been "suspended", unless you are in the Military. Those reimbursements are now taxable wage income to the non-military taxpayer, as reported on their W-2 form. These changes are in effect for the 2018 through 2025 tax years.

21) <u>The Qualified Bicycle Commuting Reimbursement Exclusion "suspended"</u>

Previously up to $20/month could be excluded from your gross income, if your employer reimbursed you for such expenses you incurred, to commute to/from work on your bicycle during that month. This change is in effect for the 2018 through 2025 tax years.

22) <u>The Tuition and Fees Deduction not extended past the 2017 tax year</u>

Previously you could deduct up to $4,000 as an Adjustment to income for the Tuition and Fees expense you paid to an Educational Institution for courses beyond high school. This was not included in the TCJA legislation to extend this income adjustment.

23) <u>The Mortgage Debt Exclusion not extended past the 2017 tax year</u>

Previously you could exclude from your Income up to $2 million of debt forgiven or canceled by your mortgage lender on a main home. Both mortgage restructuring and foreclosures qualified. This was not included in the TCJA legislation to extend this exclusion.

24) <u>The Credit for Nonbusiness Energy Property was not extended past the 2017 tax year</u>

A cumulative, lifetime, multi-year tax credit of up to $500 was available to individuals for nonbusiness energy property installed in their home. This included energy efficient residential exterior doors and windows, insulation, heat pumps, furnaces, central air conditioners, and water heaters. These were intended to make the home more energy efficient by using less fossil fuels and electricity. This was not included in the TCJA legislation to extend this credit.

25) <u>New 2019 Alimony payments no longer deducted or shown as income</u>

Alimony is no longer deducted as an Adjustment to income for the Payer, and no longer taxable as Ordinary Income to the Recipient. This TCJA tax law change applies for any new and/or modified divorce or separation agreements executed after December 31st, 2018.

26) <u>New Discharge of Student Loan Debt exclusion item added</u>

The exclusion from income resulting from the discharge of student loan debt is expanded to include discharges resulting from the death or total and permanent disability of the student. This change is in effect for the 2018 through to the 2025 tax years.

27) <u>The Professional Gambler expense deduction rules clarified</u>

Professional Gamblers can now use both losses and nonwagering gambling expenses to offset their legal Professional Gambling winnings – down to zero. They cannot use net gambling losses to offset any other Ordinary Income listed on the tax return. They can report this activity on the Schedule C (Form 1040), as a self-employed gambler. This change is in effect for the 2018 to 2025 tax years.

20) Qualified Moving Expenses are no longer deductible for most taxpayers

A Taxpayer can no longer deduct Qualified Moving Expenses related to moving to a new city for a new job, unless you are active duty in the Military and were ordered to move to a new permanent station of duty.

This Moving Expenses deduction has been "suspended" for all other, non-military taxpayers, until January 1st, 2026.

In the recent tax years if you moved for a new job, more than 50 miles away from your old job, you could deduct the Qualified Moving Expenses required to relocate yourself and your belongings to that new location. The distance between your new job and your former home had to be at least 50 miles farther than your previous employer was from that home.

The exclusion for company provided moving expense reimbursements also has been "suspended", except again for active duty Military Personnel.

If your company reimburses you for Qualified Moving Expenses, they will now report that as Wage Income on your W-2 form, and will with-hold amounts of income and employment taxes on the reimbursement.

21) The Qualified Bicycle Commuting Reimbursement Exclusion has been "suspended"

The Qualified Bicycle Commuting Reimbursement Exclusion has been "suspended" until January 1st, 2026.

Previously an employer could exclude up to $20/month from your gross income in your paycheck, if that employer reimbursed you for expenses you incurred to commute to/from work on your bicycle that month.
- Such as a new bike, safety helmet, or bike maintenance and repairs

This was allowed so long as you, the Employee, did not receive any other transit-related employee benefits such as:
- Weekly or monthly subway fare cards, bus fare cards, or car parking facility reimbursements

22) The Tuition and Fees Deduction was not extended past the 2017 tax year

Previously you could deduct up to $4,000 as an Adjustment to income for the Tuition and Fees expense you paid to an Educational Institution for courses beyond high school.

For the tax years 2018 and beyond, the Tuition and Fees Deduction is no longer available, as it was not extended past the 2017 tax year, and it was not included in the TCJA legislation.

For many tax years there had been three Education-related tax benefits. The first two listed below are still available for the 2018 tax year. The tax software calculates which is the best credit for your tax scenario.

1) **The American Opportunity Credit** for up to $2,500 per student
   - $1,500 of the credit is a nonrefundable credit to be used to help reduce your line 11 Initial Tax Obligation down to zero.
   - $1,000 of the credit is a refundable credit to increase your refund
   - You can claim this for the first four years of undergraduate college

2) **The Lifetime Learning Credit** for up to $2,000 per tax return
   - The entire $2,000 credit is a nonrefundable credit, to be used only to help reduce your line 11 Initial Tax Obligation down to zero.
   - This can be claimed for Graduate courses and Adult Learning classes you may take at an Educational Institution, for the rest of your life.
   - It can be used for undergraduate 5th year programs, like Architectural degrees, after you have taken the 4-years of the American Opportunity Credit

3) **The Tuition and Fees Deduction**, for up to $4,000 per tax return
   - This was used to reduce your Adjusted Gross Income (AGI) value
   - It is currently no longer available for the tax years after 2017

See these links from the IRS about the Education Credit tax benefits:
" Education Credits: Questions and Answers "
https://www.irs.gov/credits-deductions/individuals/education-credits-questions-and-answers
" American Opportunity Tax Credit "
https://www.irs.gov/credits-deductions/individuals/aotc
" Lifetime Learning Credit "
https://www.irs.gov/credits-deductions/individuals/llc

23) The Mortgage Debt Relief Act of 2007 exclusion was not extended past the 2017 tax year

Previously you could exclude from your Income up to $2 million of debt forgiven or canceled by your mortgage lender on a main home. Both mortgage restructuring and foreclosures qualified. The limit was $1 million for a Married Filing Separately taxpayer.

For the tax years 2018 and beyond, the Mortgage Debt Relief Act of 2007 exclusion is no longer available, as it was not extended past the 2017 tax year, and it was not included in the TCJA legislation.

Typically debt forgiveness is taxable income, unless you can prove to the IRS that you were insolvent the day before the debt was forgiven. A frequent example is when credit card debt is forgiven. Being insolvent means your liabilities exceeded your assets, the day before the debt was forgiven by the bank or financial institution. See IRS Publication 4681 - Cancelled Debts, Foreclosures, Repossessions, and Abandonments. Refer to page 6 for the Insolvency Worksheet and instructions.
https://www.irs.gov/pub/irs-pdf/p4681.pdf

The deepening mortgage crisis in 2007 necessitated the Mortgage Debt Relief Act of 2007, as many people were losing their homes. Having this large debt forgiveness value excluded from their taxable income helped many people during these difficult financial times, when they might have lost their primary residence to foreclosure.

24) The Credit for Nonbusiness Energy Property was not extended past the 2017 tax year

A cumulative, lifetime, multi-year tax credit of up to $500 was available to individuals for nonbusiness energy efficient property such as:
 • Residential exterior doors and windows, insulation, heat pumps, furnaces, central air conditioners, and water heaters.
These improvements were intended to make a Taxpayer's home more energy efficient by reducing the use of fossil fuel energy and electricity.

For the tax years 2018 and beyond, the Credit for Nonbusiness Energy Property is no longer available, as it was not extended past the 2017 tax year, and it was not included in the TCJA legislation.

25) New 2019 Alimony payments are no longer deductible for the Payer or shown as income to the Recipient

Alimony is no longer deducted as an Adjustment to income for the Payer and no longer taxable as Ordinary Income to the Recipient. This new TCJA tax law is permanent and applies for any new and/or modified divorce or separation agreements executed after December 31st, 2018.

For any previous divorce and separation agreements executed before January 1st, 2019, these previous Alimony tax law rules will still apply:
- Alimony payments are a deduction – as an Adjustment to income – for the Payer of alimony.
- Alimony payments received – are taxed as Ordinary Income – to the Recipient of alimony.

Any older pre-2019 divorce or separation agreements can be legally altered to follow the new TCJA Alimony tax law if:
- The agreement is changed after December 31st, 2018 to include additional language that:
- Acknowledges the new TCJA tax law changes regarding Alimony payments made and received.
- States in the revised agreement the subsequent Alimony payments are no longer deductible to the Payer and are no longer taxable to the Recipient.

26) New Discharge of Student Loan Debt exclusion item added

The exclusion from income resulting from the discharge of student loan debt is expanded to include discharges resulting from the death or total and permanent disability of the student.
- This new TCJA tax law covers eligible loans discharged beginning from January 1st, 2018 through to December 31st, 2025.

Currently if you work in certain job situations you can have portions of your Student Loan Debt forgiven, and excluded as taxable income.
- For example, working as a Nurse in a rural area in need of medical professionals, with the Nurse Corps Loan Repayment Program.
- Or working as an Architect for AmeriCorps to help design and build low-income housing, in communities served by AmeriCorps.

27) The Professional Gambler expense deduction rules clarified

Expenses to offset legal Professional Gambling winnings.

Professional Gamblers can now use the sum of all losses, and all expenses incurred in conjunction with gambling transactions, to offset their legal gambling winnings, down to zero. For tax years 2018 to 2025.

These are called nonwagering business expenses for Professional Gamblers, who engage in legal gambling, as their trade or business. Such as travel expenses to/from the Casino, betting fees, food & lodging, etc.

Professional Gamblers cannot use a net loss on their legal gambling activity to offset their other non-gambling related Ordinary Income.

If a Professional Gambler reports his/her gambling winnings, expenses and losses on a Schedule C (Form 1040), he/she is required to pay self-employment taxes on the net gambling winnings, if they have net profits.

Unless you are a self-employed Professional Gambler, you can only deduct gambling losses up to the amount, or extent, of your gambling winnings. You cannot use the above mentioned nonwagering expenses to offset your casual gambling winnings. You are considered a Casual Gambler. You must use and qualify for the Itemized Deductions to be able to offset your casual gambling winnings with your casual gambling losses.

It is advised you keep a contemporaneous record of your yearly gambling activity so you can accurately prove to the IRS your gambling losses and/or expenses, that you used to offset your documented winnings.

You will need this documentation if the IRS ever Audits your gambling activity. See this article from the Journal of Accountancy that explains the history of this issue for both Professional and Casual Gamblers.

"Tax Reform Law Deals Pro Gamblers A Losing Hand"
Written on October 1st, 2018 By:
 Wei-Chih Chiang, CPA, DBA; Yingxu Kuang, DBA; and Xiaobo Dong, Ph.D.
https://www.journalofaccountancy.com/issues/2018/oct/pro-gambling-net-losses.html

Chapter 5:

Tax-Advantaged Accounts and the Backdoor Roth IRA

TOPICS SUMMARY #28 to #30

28) <u>Distributions from 529 Qualified Tuition Program plans expanded</u>

The TCJA legislation added the provision that up to a $10,000 per-student yearly maximum distribution, can now be used to pay tuition for a K-12 public, private, or religious elementary or secondary school. Some K-12 Home Schooling tuition expenses may also qualify.

29) <u>ABLE account contribution limits expanded for the Disabled Beneficiary</u>

An ABLE account is a tax-advantaged savings account, in some ways similar to a Roth IRA, for people with disabilities, with an age of onset of the disability before turning 26 years of age.

Typically only a total of $15,000 per year can be contributed into an ABLE account, by people other than the disabled person – such as family, relatives or friends of the disabled beneficiary.

Now the disabled beneficiary can contribute an additional amount up to $12,060 for a total 2018 yearly maximum contribution of $27,060.

30) <u>Roth IRA recharacterization rules and the Backdoor Roth IRA explained</u>

If a Taxpayer makes in the 2018 tax year, a deductible or nondeductible contribution into a Traditional IRA, and before April 15th of the following tax year, converts that into a Roth IRA contribution – that Taxpayer cannot then convert, or recharacterize that new Roth IRA contribution back into the Traditional IRA contribution. Once the contribution is converted into a Roth IRA, it stays in the Roth IRA.

A Backdoor Roth IRA is an alternative method you can use to contribute to a Roth IRA, even though your high-income would normally prohibit that, under the direct Roth IRA contribution rules.

28) Distributions from 529 Qualified Tuition Program plans expanded

Distributions from 529 Qualified Tuition Program plans have been expanded for students below college age. This is a permanent change. The TCJA legislation added the provision that up to a $10,000 per-student yearly maximum distribution, can now be used to pay tuition for a K-12 public, private, or religious elementary or secondary school, such as:
 • Kindergarten, Grade School, Middle School or High School

These new 529 Qualified Tuition Program distribution rules are very limited as to K-12 Home Schooled tuition expenses. It is advised you inquire with your State's 529 Plan for their rules regarding using these new 529 Plan distributions for K-12 Home Schooled expenses. These may be:
 • Home Schooling Curriculum materials approve by your State
 • Printed and online instructional materials that deliver the curriculum
 • Tuition for tutors supporting educational courses in the curriculum

Previously 529 Plan distributions were only allowed to pay for tuition and some costs at post-secondary institutions, after High School such as:
 • Vocational Schools, Community Colleges, Undergraduate Degree Universities and Master Degree University programs

29) The ABLE account contribution limits expanded for the Disabled Beneficiary

The ABLE account contribution limits have been expanded for the Disabled Beneficiary. An ABLE account is a tax-advantaged savings account, in some ways similar to a Roth IRA, for people with disabilities, with an age of onset of the disability before turning 26 years of age. ABLE stands for "Achieving a Better Life Experience" from the 2014 Stephen Beck Jr., Achieving a Better Life Experience Act. The ABLE account assets normally do not affect, reduce, or limit the eligibility for the regular disability payments the person is receiving. If the beneficiary meets this age criteria and is also receiving benefits already under SSI and/or SSDI, they are automatically eligible to establish an ABLE account. ABLE accounts can provide an additional source of funds to pay yearly disability expenses of the disabled beneficiary. Distributed funds can be used to pay qualified expenses related to the disability – tax free.

There are some restrictions when the ABLE account assets grow to be over $100,000. The total annual contributions by all participating individuals into an ABLE account, including family and friends, for the 2018 tax year is $15,000, which is the 2018 Annual Gift Tax Exclusion amount.

Contributions to an ABLE account <u>are not</u> tax-deductible to the contributors or disabled beneficiary, thus one similarity to a Roth IRA.

All ABLE Account investment earnings remain untaxed providing the distributions from the account are used for Qualified Disability Expenses for the disabled beneficiary. This is another similarity to a Roth IRA, in that the distributions are not taxed.

Now due to the TCJA tax law change, the beneficiary, the disabled person, can contribute in 2018 an additional amount, being the lesser of:
- The Federal Poverty Level for a 1-person household of $12,060 or
- The disabled person's compensation for the year

This added to the previously mentioned $15,000 allows for a maximum combined 2018 yearly contribution of $27,060 into the ABLE account.

These are permanent changes that will be indexed yearly for inflation.

The disabled beneficiary can now also claim the Saver's Credit on their personal income tax return. See that IRS article below.
" Retirement Savings Contributions Credit (Saver's Credit) "
https://www.irs.gov/retirement-plans/plan-participant-employee/retirement-savings-contributions-savers-credit

Rollover funds from a 529 Plan belonging to the disabled beneficiary are now allowed without penalty, to be deposited into their ABLE account.
- This solves the previous problem of when a 529 Plan was set up at the child's birth, before the disabled condition was identified and declared permanent – such as a new permanent Autism disability. Previous to these TCJA changes, the disabled beneficiary's 529 Plan could not be rolled over into their ABLE account without penalties.
- There are some limits on the rollover amounts. Check your 529 plan.

See the website below from the ABLE National Resource Center:
http://www.ablenrc.org/about/what-are-able-accounts
See the IRS web site below for ABLE accounts:
https://www.irs.gov/government-entities/federal-state-local-governments/able-accounts-tax-benefit-for-people-with-disabilities

30) The Roth IRA recharacterization rules and the Backdoor Roth IRA explained

If a Taxpayer makes a 2018 tax year deductible or nondeductible contribution into a Traditional IRA, and before April 15th of the following tax year, converts it into a Roth IRA contribution – that Taxpayer cannot then convert, or recharacterize that new Roth IRA contribution back into the Traditional IRA contribution. Once converted into a 2018 Roth IRA, it stays in the Roth IRA. It is a permanent change in the tax law.

This rule also applies to the so-called Backdoor Roth IRA Conversions. These are still allowed by the IRS, but you cannot now "unwind" a so-called Backdoor Roth IRA conversion, made in the 2018 tax year.

A Backdoor Roth IRA conversion is a method you can use to contribute to a Roth IRA, even though your high-income would normally prohibit that, under the direct Roth IRA contribution rules as described below:
- If you are Unmarried, you must have a Modified Adjusted Gross Income (MAGI) under $135,000 to contribute to a Roth IRA for the 2018 tax year, and contributions are reduced starting at $120,000.
- If you are Married Filing Jointly, your (MAGI) must be less than $199,000 to contribute to a Roth IRA for the 2018 tax year, with the contribution reduction beginning at $189,000.
- The Married Filing Separately (MAGI) threshold is under $10,000

A Backdoor Roth IRA conversion enables a high-income Taxpayer to still contribute to a Roth IRA, even though they cannot directly make normal Roth IRA contributions per the above described income limits. You begin by making a fully nondeductible contribution into a Traditional IRA then you immediately, or soon thereafter, convert that into a Roth IRA. Congress repealed the $100K income limit on Roth Conversions in 2010.

Step 1: A Backdoor Roth IRA works by opening a Traditional IRA account and making a fully nondeductible contribution into that Traditional IRA, up to the yearly allowable contribution limit for your age.
- For example in the 2018 tax year, you can make a nondeductible IRA contribution of up to $5,500 into a Traditional IRA if you are under age 50, $6,500 at or over age 50, up to when you turn age 70 1/2.

Step 2: The nondeductible Traditional IRA contribution can then be converted immediately, the same or next day, into a Roth IRA without any of the Roth IRA income limitations – from which your high-income would normally prevent you from making a direct Roth IRA contribution.

If you keep the nondeductible contribution money in the Traditional IRA for a significant period of time, and it generates earnings, the conversion to a Backdoor Roth IRA becomes more complicated, as you have to consider the earnings into the conversion calculations, and pay taxes on those accumulated earnings.

It is less complicated if you complete both transactions in the same calendar tax year. This makes the reporting of the two transactions to the IRS appear in the same tax year, on that tax year's tax return.
- You will receive the IRA distribution Form 1099-R from your Brokerage showing the distribution from your Traditional IRA that was then converted to your Roth IRA.
- You will receive the IRA Contribution Information Form 5498 that shows the nondeductible contribution you made into the Traditional IRA, and the amount that was then converted into the Roth IRA.
- The nondeductible contribution will be reported on the Form 8606

Your Brokerage can help you with this so-called Backdoor Roth IRA conversion. They can assist you in setting up both types of IRA accounts.

Recommendation #1: when you convert IRA moneys into the Roth IRA
Be aware of the Pro-Rata Rule if you own multiple Traditional IRA accounts and you have made pre-tax and after-tax contributions.
- Pre-tax contributions, or deductible contributions, into a Traditional IRA account, qualify you for the IRA Deduction on your yearly tax return. This is now shown on the line 32 of the Schedule 1 form.
- After-tax contributions, or nondeductible contributions, do not qualify you for the IRA Deduction on your tax return. They add to what is called the "Basis" of the IRA account. This "Basis" is not taxed at retirement after age 59 1/2 when you might begin IRA distributions.
  - You report nondeductible contributions yearly on the Form 8606

The nondeductible contributions you made into the Traditional IRA accounts are not taxed when you convert that to a Roth IRA.

The deductible contributions you made into the Traditional IRA accounts plus any accumulated earnings, are taxed when converted to a Roth IRA.

The Pro-Rata Rule formula below accounts for these two types of contributions plus accumulated earnings in the Traditional IRA accounts. It calculates as the amount of the Roth conversion that is taxable.
{ [Total Pre-Tax Contributions + Earnings, in all IRAs on Dec. 31st] divided by [Total Value of all IRAs on Dec. 31st] } multiplied by [Amount of money converted to the Roth IRA].

<u>For Example - assume these values as of Dec. 31st of the tax year</u>
Let us assume you have a total of $100,000 of contributions plus earnings in all of your Traditional IRA accounts with $10,000 of that money being nondeductible contributions – considered after-tax contributions.

Therefore $90,000 of the IRA moneys came from the pre-tax deductible contributions and the subsequent earnings. You received a tax benefit as a Traditional IRA Deduction on your yearly tax returns, for each of the tax years you made these pre-tax Traditional IRA contributions.

So $90,000 (pre-tax contributions + earnings) divided by $100,000 (total of all IRA accounts) equals 90%. Therefore you will owe taxes on 90% of any money you convert into a Roth IRA from these Traditional IRAs.

<u>Taxes Owed on the Earnings accrued in the Traditional IRA account(s)</u>

If you earn profits in a Traditional IRA account funded only with pre-tax deductible contributions, and then you convert that into a Roth IRA, you will pay tax on the entire conversion amount. That entire distribution is categorized as Ordinary Income when you convert into the Roth IRA.

If you earn profits in a Traditional IRA account with a mixture of pre-tax and after-tax contributions, you pay tax on the Roth conversion on the amount above the after-tax, non-deductible contribution values.

<u>For Example - consider this Traditional IRA scenario over a 3-yr period:</u>
- In year one you made a $5,000 pre-tax contribution into the Traditional IRA. This would give you an IRA Deduction on your tax return.

- In year two you made a $5,000 after-tax contribution into the Traditional IRA account. This would be a nondeductible contribution and is considered as non-taxable "Basis" in the IRA.
  - This nondeductible contribution does not qualify you for the Traditional IRA Deduction on your tax return. It adds to the total funds in the Traditional IRA and creates what is called "Basis" in the IRA.
  - This is reported to the IRS on Form 8606 on that year's tax return.

- On December 31st of year three the account is worth $11,000.
  - This $11,000 represents $1,000 in earnings in addition to the $10,000 in combined IRA contributions from the previous two tax years. You still have that $5,000 non-taxable "Basis" in this Traditional IRA.

- When you convert this entire Traditional IRA into a Roth IRA on December 31st of the 3rd year, you would use the following formula:

  - Your "Basis" in the IRA is still $5,000 from the nondeductible after-tax contribution that you made in year two.
  - $11,000 (total IRA value) minus $5,000 (Basis) equals $6,000
  - So you must pay taxes on $6,000 as Ordinary Income with the Roth conversion when you converted this entire Traditional IRA account.

Recommendation #2: seek Professional help for complicated conversions

Software like TurboTax™ will help you calculate this Backdoor Roth IRA conversion, using the Pro-Rata Rules if required. But it is a somewhat involved calculation and you will reap benefits if you are familiar with the conversion rules as described in this Topic explanation.

As an IRS Enrolled Agent I would strongly suggest you seek the advice of a tax professional if you have multiple traditional IRA accounts with pre-tax contributions and/or you have any after-tax, nondeductible contribution "Basis" in any of those IRA accounts – and you are attempting to complete a partial or full Backdoor Roth IRA conversion.

An Enrolled Agent, an Accountant, or a Tax Lawyer can provide you valuable advice how to best report the Backdoor Roth IRA transaction on that year's tax return, to satisfy the strict IRS reporting requirements for such a scenario.

See the links below from the IRS:
"IRA FAQs - Rollovers and Roth Conversions"
https://www.irs.gov/retirement-plans/retirement-plans-faqs-regarding-iras-rollovers-and-roth-conversions
Pub 590-A: Contributions to Individual Retirement Arrangements (IRAs)
https://www.irs.gov/pub/irs-pdf/p590a.pdf
Form 8606 - Nondeductible IRAs
https://www.irs.gov/pub/irs-prior/f8606--2018.pdf
Form 1099-R - Distributions from Pensions, Annuities, Retirement or Profit-Sharing Plans, IRAs, Insurance Contracts, etc.
https://www.irs.gov/pub/irs-prior/f1099r--2018.pdf
Form 5498 - IRA Contribution Information
https://www.irs.gov/pub/irs-prior/f5498--2018.pdf

Chapter 6:

The Affordable Care Act changes

TOPICS SUMMARY #31 to #32

31) <u>The Penalty Tax for not having Health Insurance still in effect for 2018</u>

The Penalty Tax is still in effect for not having Qualified Health Insurance for all 12-months of the 2018 tax year.

The Penalty is then reduced to Zero for tax years 2019 and beyond.

The Premium Tax Credit and the Advanced Premium Tax Credit are still available to certain income taxpayers to subsidize, or help pay for, their monthly health insurance premiums they incurred for qualified health insurance policies purchased on the State or National Marketplace Health Insurance Exchanges, aka "Obamacare" policies.

In general, to be eligible for the Premium Tax Credit, your household income must be at least 100% – but not more than 400% – of the federal poverty line value for your family size. See the chart below.

©2019 Internal Revenue Service - from the 2018 Form 8962 Instructions, page 7

Table 1-1. **Federal Poverty Line for the 48 Contiguous States and the District of Columbia**	
IF your Family Size* from Form 8962, line 1, was . . .	THEN enter the amount below on Form 8962, line 4 . . .
1	$12,060
2	$16,240
3	$20,420
4	$24,600
5	$28,780
6	$32,960
7	$37,140
8	$41,320

32) <u>The two high-income Affordable Care Act taxes have been retained</u>

The 3.8% Net Investment Income Tax – for high-earner investment income, has been retained.

The 0.9% Additional Medicare Tax – for high-earner salaried employees and/or self-employed individuals, has been retained.

31) The Penalty Tax for not having Qualified Health Insurance is still in effect for the 2018 tax year

The Penalty Tax for not having Qualified Health Insurance for all 12-months of the 2018 tax year has remained. This is referred to as the Individual Mandate, which was part of the Affordable Care Act, to induce people to buy health insurance, to even out the risk pools between healthy and sick people. The penalty payments generate revenue to help pay for the Premium Tax Credits, which subsidize the monthly health insurance premiums for certain income taxpayers, who purchase health insurance through the Marketplace Health Insurance Exchanges.[3]

Taxpayers still face this penalty tax payment, called the Individual Shared Responsibility Payment, for the 2018 tax year, if they did not have Qualified Health Insurance for all 12-months of the 2018 tax year.
- The 2018 tax year penalty is calculated as the greater of $695 per uninsured adult in the household, $347.50 per uninsured child in the household (up to a maximum of $2,085 per family), or 2.5% of your household income above the filing threshold for your filing status.
- The 2018 tax year is the last year you have to pay this penalty tax.
The yearly penalty tax amount, as described above, is then pro-rated for only the months you did not have Qualified Health Insurance.

For Example: Let us assume you had the following situation in 2018 regarding your health insurance coverage. You used the Single filing status.
- You did not have the required Qualified Health Insurance for 3 months in the 2018 tax year for the months of July, August and September.
- Your income above the tax filing threshold for your filing status, subject to the Individual Shared Responsibility Payment, was $60,000.
- Your yearly penalty is the greater of $695 or 2.5% of your income above your tax filing threshold. (2.5%) times ($60,000) equals $1,500.
- Your maximum penalty could then be $1,500 for the entire year, if you didn't have health insurance for all 12-months of the 2018 tax year.
- The higher 2.5% penalty based on your 2018 income is $1,500 for the entire year, which works out to be $125/month.
- So your 3-month penalty would be 3 * $125 = $375.

The TCJA legislation reduced this penalty tax amount to Zero, for tax years 2019 and beyond. It remains at Zero until changed by Congress.

[3] https://www.taxpolicycenter.org/briefing-book/what-tax-changes-did-affordable-care-act-make

32) The two high-income Affordable Care Act taxes have been retained

The two Affordable Care Act taxes have been retained – for high-earner's investment and salary/self-employed income. These taxes were part of the Affordable Care Act, to generate revenue to fund the Premium Tax Credit subsidies that certain income taxpayers receive to help them pay for health insurance policies purchased through the Marketplace Health Insurance Exchanges.[3]

The 3.8% Net Investment Income Tax – for high-earner investment income, has been retained with the TCJA legislation. Per the IRS:[4]
- "If an individual has income from investments, the individual may be subject to net investment income tax. Taxpayers are liable for a 3.8 percent Net Investment Income Tax on the lesser of their net investment income, or the amount by which their modified adjusted gross income exceeds this income threshold amount based on filing status.
  - Married Filing Jointly — $250,000,
  - Married Filing Separately — $125,000,
  - Single or Head of Household — $200,000, or
  - Qualifying Widow(er) with a dependent child — $250,000
- Net Investment Income includes but is not limited to: interest, dividends, capital gain, rental/royalty income, and non-qualified annuities."

The 0.9% Additional Medicare Tax – for high-earner salaried employees, and self-employed, has been retained with the TCJA legislation. Per IRS:[5]
- "An individual is liable for the 0.9% Additional Medicare Tax if the individual's wages, compensation, or self-employment income (together with that of his or her spouse if filing a joint return) exceed the threshold amounts for the individual's filing status."
  - Married Filing Jointly — $250,000,
  - Married Filing Separately — $125,000,
  - Single or Head of Household — $200,000, or
  - Qualifying Widow(er) with a dependent child — $200,000

The Premium Tax Credit and the Advanced Premium Tax Credit have remained after the TCJA legislation for tax years 2018 and beyond.

[3] https://www.taxpolicycenter.org/briefing-book/what-tax-changes-did-affordable-care-act-make

[4] https://www.irs.gov/newsroom/questions-and-answers-on-the-net-investment-income-tax

[5] https://www.irs.gov/businesses/small-businesses-self-employed/questions-and-answers-for-the-additional-medicare-tax

54

Chapter 7:

High-Earner income changes

TOPICS SUMMARY #33 to #36

33) Far fewer taxpayers will be subject to the
Alternative Minimum Tax (AMT)

The Alternative Minimum Tax (AMT) exemption amounts have increased significantly such that far fewer upper middle income taxpayers will have this AMT tax obligation in 2018 through to 2025.
The exemption phase-out range amounts have also increased which
will help taxpayers have a lower AMT obligation on their tax return.

34) The Kiddie Tax revised to no longer use the Parent's marginal tax rate

The so-called Kiddie Tax was revised to no longer use the Parent's
marginal tax rate to calculate the tax obligation on the Child's Unearned Income – above the defined $2,100 threshold.

The Child's Unearned Income above $2,100 subject to the Kiddie Tax
will now be taxed using the Trust and Estate tax rates.

35) New Deferral of Income for Private Company Stock Option Plans

Tax Code Section 83(i) Election allows an employee to defer, for income tax purposes, the inclusion of income due to exercising certain
Private Company stock options and/or restricted stock units (RSUs).

36) Estate/Gift Tax Exemptions doubled and $15,000/yr Gift Tax Exclusion

For Estates of decedents dying and gifts made after December 31st,
2017 and before January 1st, 2026, the base estate and gift tax exemption amount has more than doubled. The Annual Gift Tax Exclusion amount for the 2018 tax year has been increased to $15,000.

33) Far fewer taxpayers will be subject to the Alternative Minimum Tax (AMT)

The Alternative Minimum Tax (AMT) exemption amounts have increased significantly such that far fewer upper middle income taxpayers will have this AMT tax obligation. The exemption phase-out range amounts have also increased, which will help taxpayers have a lower AMT obligation on their 2018 through 2025 tax returns. See the table below.

AMT Tables based on the tables in TheTaxBook™, redrawn by the Author for clarity.

2017 AMT Exemption Amounts

Single & Head of Household Filing Status $54,300

Married Filing Jointly|Qualifying Widow(er) Filing Status $84,500

Married Filing Separately Filing Status $42,250

The AMT exemption amount is reduced by 25% of the amount by which a taxpayer's AMTI exceeds the beginning of the phase-out range.

2017 AMT Phase-Out Ranges

Single & Head of Household .... $120,700 to $337,900

Married Filing Jointly|Qualifying Widow(er) .... $160,900 to $498,900

Married Filing Separately Filing Status .... $80,450 to $249,450

2018 AMT Exemption Amounts

Single & Head of Household Filing Status $70,300

Married Filing Jointly|Qualifying Widow(er) Filing Status $109,400

Married Filing Separately Filing Status $54,700

2018 AMT Phase-Out Ranges

Single & Head of Household .... $500,000 to $781,200

Married Filing Jointly|Qualifying Widow(er) .. $1,000,000 to $1,437,600

Married Filing Separately Filing Status .... $500,000 to $718,800

These amounts are indexed each year for inflation after 2018.

The Tax Policy Center estimates that only about 200,000 tax filers are expected to owe the AMT in 2018 – much lower than the 5.25 million who they estimate would have owed under the old tax law.[6] The AMT was enacted in 1969 after 155 higher-income taxpayers were identified as paying no taxes on their 1967 tax returns, with AGIs above $200K.
See this Wikipedia article for the early and current history of the AMT:
https://en.wikipedia.org/wiki/Alternative_minimum_tax

[6] https://www.taxpolicycenter.org/model-estimates/baseline-alternative-minimum-tax-amt-tables-oct-2018/t18-0145-aggregate-amt

34) The Kiddie Tax was revised to no longer use the Parent's marginal tax rate

The so-called Kiddie Tax was revised to no longer use the Parent's marginal tax rate to calculate the tax obligation on the Child's Unearned Income – above the defined $2,100 threshold. Using the Parent's marginal tax rate has been "suspended" after December 31st, 2017, and before January 1st, 2026. The Child's Unearned Income above $2,100 subject to the Kiddie Tax is now taxed using the Trust and Estate tax rates.

The Kiddie Tax was enacted in 1986 to prevent Parents from shifting their Investment Income gains from their higher tax bracket, to their Child's lower tax bracket – by moving their Investments into a Child's investment or bank account.

It is a tax on a Child's Investment and other Unearned Income over a defined threshold of $2,100. The Kiddie Tax affects children under the age of 18, or children who are full-time students under the age of 24.

The Child must have a tax filing requirement, to be subject to the Kiddie Tax. See page 3 in the Pub. 929 below for an explanation of when a dependent is required to file a tax return. The Child's Unearned Investment Income can be reported in one of two ways on a 2018 tax return.

Option #1: On the Child's tax return - as the Kiddie Tax
- If the Child's interest, dividends and other Unearned Income total more than $2,100, the amount of that Unearned Income above $2,100 will now be subject to tax rates applicable to Trusts and Estates.
- The Child's Unearned Income above the $2,100 threshold was previously taxed using the Parent's marginal tax rate.
- The unmarried Child's Earned Income is taxed using a modified Single tax rate table. Earned Income could be from a summer job, etc.

See this IRS form and its instructions to report this Kiddie Tax income:
Form 8615 (2018)_Tax for Certain Children Who Have Unearned Income
https://www.irs.gov/pub/irs-pdf/f8615.pdf
Form 8615 (2018)_Instructions
https://www.irs.gov/pub/irs-pdf/i8615.pdf
See this IRS Publication 929, Tax Rules for Children and Dependents
https://www.irs.gov/pub/irs-pdf/p929.pdf

Option #2: On the Parent's tax return

- If the Child only has interest, dividend, or capital gain distribution income below $10,500, the Parents can elect to report that Child's Unearned Investment Income on their tax return. The Child would then not be required to file their own tax return.
- The Child must be under the age of 19 at the end of the year or under the age of 24 at the end of the year if a full-time student.
- The Child must have a tax filing requirement for the 2018 tax year
- Income between $0 up to $1,050 is not taxed
- Income between $1,050 up to $2,100 will be taxed at 10%.
- Income above $2,100 to under $10,500 is taxed at the Parent's tax rate.

You will use the IRS Form "8814_Parents' Election To Report Child's Interest and Dividends" to report the Child's income on your tax return.
https://www.irs.gov/pub/irs-pdf/f8814.pdf

This is a rather complicated subject, but as always, the tax software will help you calculate the Kiddie Tax. Or your Paid Preparer can explain the Kiddie Tax implications for your particular tax scenario.

See the tables below that illustrate the Kiddie Tax rate changes using the Trust and Estate Tax Rates.

Trust and Estate Tax Rates for 2018

Use the following tax rates to compute the Kiddie Tax for 2018 thru 2025.

2018 Ordinary Income Tax Rates for Trusts and Estates

10% tax bracket	$0 - $2,550
24% tax bracket	$2,551 - $9,150
35% tax bracket	$9,151 - $12,500
37% tax bracket	$12,501 and above

2018 Long-Term Capital Gains and Qualified Dividends Tax Rates for Trusts and Estates

0% tax bracket	$0 - $2,600
15% tax bracket	$2,601 - $12,700
20% tax bracket	$12,701 and above

2018 Kiddie Tax - Unearned Income

The portion of a child's investment income that exceeds $2,100 is taxed at the brackets and rates for trusts and estates.

- The first $2,550 is taxed at 10%
- The next $6,600 is taxed at 24%
- The next $3,350 is taxed at 35%
- Any amount beyond that is taxed at 37%

Trust & Estate Tax Rate tables from the blog at
https://www.dsb-cpa.com/new-law-revamps-the-kiddie-tax/
Kiddie Tax Rate Table from TurboTax™ blog

Both were redrawn by the Author for Clarity

35) New Deferral of Income for
Private Company Stock Option Plans

The deferral of income reporting for Private Company Stock Option Plans using the new Internal Revenue Code Section 83(i) Election.

This new TCJA tax law allows an employee to defer, for income tax purposes, the inclusion of income due to exercising certain Private Company stock options and/or restricted stock units (RSUs). This is a new IRC Code section and is a permanent change in the tax law.

Under the newly enacted Internal Revenue Code Section 83(i), in cases where "qualified stock" is transferred to a "qualified employee", the employee may elect to defer the recognition of taxable income on the transfer for up to five years. For stock options exercised post 12/31/2017.

By electing to defer the income reporting component of the stock option exercise event, the taxpayer can defer the taxes usually due on the reported income resulting from the exercise of the stock options.

This Section 83(i) Election is only applicable to employees of Private Companies whose stock is not currently publicly traded on an established U.S. stock exchange. Per the Investopedia definition:[7]
- "A private company is a firm held under private ownership. Private companies may issue stock and have shareholders, but their shares do not trade on public exchanges and are not issued through an initial public offering (IPO)."

There are strict and very detailed reporting requirements for the Private Company to offer this sort of Section 83(i) income deferral benefit to their employees.

It is recommended you consult the Accountant, Lawyer or Brokerage Firm that setup your Private Company Stock Option Plan for advice on implementing this new Section 83(i) Election benefit, for your employees. See this IRS Notice 2018-97 for the Section 83(i) Election benefit rules and implementation details:
https://www.irs.gov/pub/irs-drop/n-18-97.pdf

[7] https://www.investopedia.com/terms/p/privatecompany.asp

36) The Estate and Gift Tax Exemption amounts doubled and the $15,000/year Gift Tax Exclusion amount

For Estates of decedents dying and gifts made after December 31st, 2017 and before January 1st, 2026:

The Estate and Gift Tax Exemption amount has more than doubled to:
- $11.18 million in 2018 for unmarried taxpayers, up from an amount of $5.49 million in 2017
- $22.36 million in 2018 for married taxpayers, up from an amount of $10.98 million in 2017
- Amounts will be adjusted for inflation for the tax years after 2018

The Generation-Skipping Transfer Tax Exemption amounts have also been increased to these same levels.

The Annual Gift Tax Exclusion amount has increased to $15,000 for the 2018 tax year. This is the amount an individual can give as a non-taxable cash or property gift to another individual, without having the tax filing obligation to report that $15,000 gift on a 2018 Gift Tax Return.

A Taxpayer can give <u>one</u> of these yearly $15,000 gifts to as many individuals as they desire, and not be required to file a Gift Tax Return.

If you give a gift of property, the fair market value (FMV) must be the same $15,000 or less, to avoid the Gift Tax Return obligation. For example, you gave a 5-yr old car to a friend. Get it appraised for the FMV.

The person who receives the $15,000 cash or property gift is not required to report that as cash income or the property value on their 2018 tax return, or pay income taxes on the amount. It is truly a gift!

If you resell the gifted property, you consider the adjusted cost basis value that the donor had, to calculate your gain or loss on the sale. Gifted real estate has other more involved rules if you sell the property.

See this article from the Tax Policy Center:
"How do the estate, gift, and generation-skipping transfer taxes work? "
https://www.taxpolicycenter.org/briefing-book/how-do-estate-gift-and-generation-skipping-transfer-taxes-work

Chapter 8:

The new 20% Qualified Business Income deduction

37) The new 20% Qualified Business Income deduction

This new 20% Qualified Business Income (QBI) deduction can benefit Taxpayers with business income from a Sole Proprietorship, Single-Member LLC and Pass-Through business entities, like a Partnership.

The following four less common Qualified Business Income sources not covered in this book are.
• Qualified Business Income that a Trust and/or Estate can earn
• Dividend Income from a Real Estate Investment Trust (REIT)
• Income from a Publicly Traded Partnership (PTP)
• Dividend Income from an Agricultural or Horticultural Cooperative

This Chapter describes the QBI Income for two Sole Proprietorships.

This new Internal Revenue Code Section 199A was created to give these smaller unincorporated businesses a tax benefit deduction, similar in effect to the lowered flat 21% tax rate on Corporations.

This new deduction can be up to 20% of their Qualified Business Income. There are Taxable Income Limitation thresholds and other limitations that can reduce or entirely eliminate the QBI deduction.

The QBI deduction is subtracted from the Form 1040 postcard line 7 Adjusted Gross Income value to reduce the line 10 Taxable Income.

This chapter will illustrate six examples to explain three typical QBI business scenarios that a Sole Proprietor Plumber and a Sole Proprietor Accountant will encounter to calculate their QBI deductions.

The examples explain what the QBI deductions will be for the Plumber and Accountant when their Taxable Income is Below, Above and Between the Taxable Income phase-out ranges.

37) The new 20% Qualified Business Income deduction

This new deduction is described in the new Internal Revenue Code (IRC) Section 199A. You can read the text for the current IRC Section 199A at this Cornell Law School link.

https://www.law.cornell.edu/uscode/text/26/199A

This QBI Deduction is in effect for the 2018 through 2025 tax years.

This new Internal Revenue Code Section 199A was created to give these smaller unincorporated businesses a tax benefit deduction, similar in effect to the newly lowered flat 21% tax rate on Corporations. The Corporate tax rate had been graduated from a low of 15% up to 35%.

Congress intended to encourage these smaller unincorporated businesses to grow as they create hundreds of thousands of new jobs each year. Lower business taxes are viewed by some Members of Congress as an incentive for businesses to expand, to invest in new plants and equipment, to hire new workers, and to grow. According to the U.S. Bureau of Labor Statistics, since the end of the Great Recession in 2009, small businesses with fewer than 500 employees, have created 62 percent of all net new private-sector jobs.[8]

Many unincorporated business entities are so-called Pass-Through entities because the business income, expenses, deductions, losses, etc. are allocated through to their Partners, Shareholders and Members - to be listed on those business owner's U.S. Individual Income Tax Return.

These Pass-Through business entity types may include:
- Partnerships
- S-Corporations (S-Corps)
- Limited Liability Companies (LLCs) treated as a Multi-Member LLC such as a Partnership LLC

These particular business entities do not file a normal Corporation tax return. They file informational tax returns related to their entity type with the IRS that report the entity income, expenses, etc. as they were allocated to each business owner. The owners then receive a K-1 form.

Sole Proprietorships and Single-Member LLCs also can benefit from the QBI deduction if they report a net profit on the Schedule C (Form 1040) that reports the income and expenses incurred for their business.

[8] https://www.sba.gov/sites/default/files/Job_Creation_fact_sheet_FINAL_0.pdf

These four less common Qualified Business Income sources are not covered in this book. This Chapter only describes two Sole Proprietorships.
- Qualified Business Income that a Trust and/or Estate can earn
- Dividend income from a Real Estate Investment Trust (REIT)
- Income from a Publicly Traded Partnership (PTP)
- Dividend income from an Agricultural or Horticultural Cooperative

A Sole Proprietorship and/or Single-Member LLC reports all their business income and "Ordinary & Necessary" expenses on the Schedule C (Form 1040), which is included along with their Form 1040 postcard form.

A Partnership, S-Corp and LLC Partnership file informational tax returns that report the entity income, expenses, etc. to the IRS. They then issue K-1 reporting forms to the Partners, S-Corp Shareholders or LLC Members to allocate the income, expenses, etc. of the business entity that then "passes-through" and is assigned to these individuals. Thus the term Pass-Through entities. These individuals then report that Pass-Through information from their K-1 forms, on their Individual tax returns. 2018 K-1 forms now show the properly allocated QBI information.

This new deduction can be up to 20% of a business' Qualified Business Income. There are Taxable Income Limitation thresholds and other limitations that can reduce or even eliminate the QBI deduction.

The lower values of the Taxable Income Limitation thresholds are:
- $157,500 of Taxable Income for unmarried Individuals or a Married Filing Separately taxpayer
- $315,000 of Taxable Income if filing a Married Filing Jointly return
Taxable Income below these levels could allow the full 20% Qualified Business Income deduction if all the QBI deduction rules have been met.
For Example:
A Married Filing Jointly Sole Proprietor Plumber could possibly qualify for this additional 20% deduction of his Qualified Business Income, if he and his wife's joint Taxable Income is below that $315,000 level.

The QBI deduction begins to phase-out above these lower levels and is limited or can be eliminated above the top of these phase-out ranges:
- For an Unmarried or Married Filing Separately taxpayer the phase-out range is between $157,500 and $207,500, a $50,000 difference.
- For a Married Filing Jointly taxpayer the phase-out range is between $315,000 and $415,000, a $100,000 difference.

The treatment of the QBI deduction begins to be limited when the Taxable Income is <u>Between</u> and/or <u>Above</u> these income thresholds, depending if the business is a "Specified Service Trade or Business" (SSTB) as compared to a non-SSTB business referred to as a "Qualified Trade or Business". Refer to the Examples #1 through #6 beginning on page 66 for an explanation of these differences when an SSTB is involved.

A "Specified Service Trade or Business" SSTB, per the IRS, is any trade or business providing professional or personal services in the fields of:
- health, law, accounting, actuarial science, performing arts, consulting, athletics, financial services, and brokerage services
- or any other trade or business where the taxpayer receives fees, compensation, or other income for endorsing products or services, for the use of the taxpayer's image, likeness, name, signature, voice, trademark or any other symbols associated with the taxpayer's identity, or for appearing at an event or on radio, television, or another media format. An example would be Cindy Crawford, the model.
- In addition, the trades or businesses of investing and investment management, trading or dealing in securities, partnership interests, or commodities – are a "Specified Service Trade or Business" SSTB.
- Architects and Engineers are exempt from this category and are not classified as a "Specified Service Trade or Business" SSTB.

This QBI Deduction is shown on line 9 of the new single-page Form 1040 postcard. It is subtracted from the line 7 Adjusted Gross Income (AGI) after the line 8 Standard Deduction or Itemized Deductions have been taken into consideration and also subtracted from the line 7 AGI. It helps reduce the Taxable Income value shown on line 10 of the new single-page Form 1040 postcard. It cannot reduce this line 10 Taxable Income value below zero. It is not considered a refundable deduction.

There are additional possible limitations on the QBI Deduction based on:
- <u>The Taxable Income Limitation</u>, which uses these values:
  - (Taxable Income) minus (Net Capital Gain)
- <u>The Wage and Asset Limitation</u>, which uses these values:
  - W-2 Wages Paid and the Unadjusted Basis of Qualified Property
- Businesses that are a "<u>Specified Service Trade or Business</u>" SSTB
For the simple example of the Plumber mentioned above:
His final QBI deduction would be the <u>lesser</u> of:
- 20% of the Qualified Business Income or
- 20% of the Plumber's [(Taxable Income) minus (Net Capital Gain)]

For Example: Consider the following simple scenario for this Plumber:
- This example omits the mention of subtractions from QBI income of self-employment tax, health insurance, and retirement contributions.
- The Married Filing Jointly (MFJ) Sole Proprietor Plumber mentioned above had $78,000 of Qualified Business Income.
- The combined Taxable Income with his wife is $185,000 including $23,000 of Net Capital Gain. This is before the QBI deduction.
  - The Net Capital Gain is ("Net Capital Gain" + Qualified Dividends)
  - The term "Net Capital Gain" is defined as the excess of the net long-term capital gain for the taxable year over the net short-term capital loss for the taxable year as shown on the Schedule D.
- They are below the $315,000 lower limit on Taxable Income for the MFJ couple, as the Taxable Income is $185,000 before QBI deduction
- The potential simple Normal QBI Deduction would then be:
  - ($78,000 Qualified Business Income) times 20% equals $15,600
- The Taxable Income Limitation would be:
  - 20% of [(Taxable Income) minus (Net Capital Gain)]
  - ($185,000 minus $23,000) = ($162,000) times 20% equals $32,400.
- Therefore the simple Normal QBI deduction of $15,600 is the lesser of the Taxable Income Limitation of $32,400.
- The line 9 final QBI Deduction on the new Form 1040 postcard would then be $15,600 in this example - the lower of the two values.
- This could help reduce their final line 10 Taxable Income potentially down to zero, by subtracting this $15,600 QBI Deduction amount.

See "2018 QBI Deduction-Simplified Worksheet" on page 37, from the IRS form 1040 Instructions used to calculate this simple QBI Deduction: https://www.irs.gov/pub/irs-pdf/i1040gi.pdf

If you self-prepare your own tax return using software like TurboTax™ the software interview will guide you through the process of qualifying for this new 20% QBI deduction. If you hire a Paid Preparer to complete your tax return, they will advise you about this deduction and their professional software will handle all the applicable calculations to qualify you for the 20% QBI deduction.

See the six Examples on the following pages with the accompanying explanations and calculations – to help illustrate some of the more complex scenarios under which a Sole Proprietor business owner can take advantage of this new 20% QBI deduction. The examples explain the three scenarios each for the Plumber and for an Accountant. The Accountant is considered to be a "Specified Service Trade or Business" SSTB.

Example #1: The Sole Proprietor Plumber where their Married Filing Jointly combined Taxable Income is **Below** the phase-out range between $315,000 up to $415,000 for their Married Filing Jointly status.

Example #2: The Sole Proprietor Plumber where their Married Filing Jointly combined Taxable Income is **Above** the phase-out range between $315,000 up to $415,000 for their Married Filing Jointly status.

Example #3: The Sole Proprietor Plumber where their Married Filing Jointly combined Taxable Income is **Between** the phase-out range between $315,000 up to $415,000 for their Married Filing Jointly status.

The Plumber **is not** a "Specified Service Trade or Business" SSTB.

He is considered to be a "**Qualified Trade or Business**".

Example #4: A wife of a married couple who owns and operates a Sole Proprietor Accounting business. Her combined Taxable Income with her husband is **Below** the phase-out range between $315,000 up to $415,000 for their Married Filing Jointly status.

Example #5: A wife of a married couple who owns and operates a Sole Proprietor Accounting business. Her combined Taxable Income with her husband is **Above** the phase-out range between $315,000 up to $415,000 for their Married Filing Jointly status.

Example #6: A wife of a married couple who owns and operates a Sole Proprietor Accounting business. Her combined Taxable Income with her husband is **Between** the phase-out range between $315,000 up to $415,000 for their Married Filing Jointly status.

Her Accounting firm **is** a "**Specified Service Trade or Business**" SSTB.

An SSTB business owner **does not** receive any QBI deduction when their Taxable Income is **Above** the upper level of the Taxable Income phase-out levels.

Example #1: The Sole Proprietor Plumber where their Married Filing Jointly combined Taxable Income is **Below** the phase-out range between $315,000 up to $415,000 for their Married Filing Jointly status.

The Facts of the Example:
1) The Plumber files as Married Filing Jointly with his wife
2) Their combined Taxable Income before QBI deduction is $185,000
   • Including $23,000 of Net Capital Gain
3) Their Taxable Income is **Below** the $315,000 lower value of the Taxable Income phase-out levels between $315,000 to $415,000
4) The Plumber's business showed a $78,000 net profit for the year
   • He has a deduction of $5,511 of 1/2 of his self-employment tax
5) The Plumber is considered to be a "Qualified Trade or Business", not the more restrictive "Specified Service Trade or Business" SSTB.
6) They received their family health insurance through his wife's job, so the Plumber has no self-employed health insurance deduction.
7) The Plumber did not contribute to a self-employed retirement plan.

The Rules to Calculate this Qualified Business Income (QBI) Deduction:
1) The QBI Deduction will be the <u>lower</u> of these two values
   • The Normal QBI Deduction
     • 20% of his [(Qualified Business Income)]
     • 20% of his [(Net Business Profit) minus (1/2 SE Tax)]
   • The Taxable Income Limitation
     • 20% of [(Taxable Income) minus (Net Capital Gain)]

The Calculations:
1) The Normal QBI Deduction
   • 20% of his [(Qualified Business Income)]
   • 20% of his [(Net Business Profit) minus (1/2 SE Tax)]
   • 20% times [($78,000) minus ($5,511)]
   • 20% times $72,489 equals <u>$14,498</u>
2) The Taxable Income Limitation
   • 20% of their [(Taxable Income) minus (Net Capital Gain)]
   • 20% times [($185,000 minus $23,000)]
   • 20% times ($162,000) equals <u>$32,400</u>

The Final Line 9 Qualified Business Income Deduction is $14,498
This is the <u>lesser</u> value of:

The Normal QBI Deduction of $14,498 or
The Taxable Income Limitation of $32,400

Example #2: The Sole Proprietor Plumber where their Married Filing Jointly combined Taxable Income is **Above** the phase-out range between $315,000 up to $415,000 for their Married Filing Jointly status.

The Facts of the Example:

1) The Plumber files as Married Filing Jointly with his wife
2) Their combined Taxable Income before QBI deduction is $525,000
   • Including $23,000 of Net Capital Gain
3) Their Taxable Income is **Above** the higher $415,000 value of the Taxable Income phase-out levels between $315,000 to $415,000
4) The Plumber's business showed a $450,000 net profit for the year
   • He has a deduction of $13,987 of 1/2 of his self-employment tax
5) The Plumber is considered to be a "Qualified Trade or Business", not the more restrictive "Specified Service Trade or Business" SSTB.
6) The Plumber had no deductions for self-employed health insurance or for a contribution to a self-employed retirement plan
7) The Plumber has four employees as apprentice plumbers
   • The Plumber paid $150,000 in W-2 Wages to the four employees
8) The Plumber has four pickup trucks and plumbing tools as Assets
   • The UBIA (Unadjusted Basis Immediately after Acquisition) of the four pickup trucks and plumbing tools is $200,000

The Rules to Calculate this Qualified Business Income (QBI) Deduction:

1) The QBI Deduction will be the lower of these three values
   • The Normal QBI Deduction
     • 20% of his [(Qualified Business Income)]
     • 20% of his [(Net Business Profit) minus (1/2 SE Tax)]
   • The Taxable Income Limitation
     • 20% of [(Taxable Income) minus (Net Capital Gain)]
   • The Wage and Asset Limitation, which is the Greater value of:
     • 50% of the employee Wages the business paid, or
     • (25% of the Wages) + (2.5% of the UBIA of the Business Assets)

The Calculations:

1) The Normal QBI Deduction
   - 20% of his [(Qualified Business Income)]
   - 20% of his [(Net Business Profit) minus (1/2 SE Tax)]
   - 20% times [($450,000) minus ($13,987)]
   - 20% times $436,013 equals $87,203
2) The Taxable Income Limitation
   - 20% of their [(Taxable Income) minus (Net Capital Gain)]
   - 20% times [($525,000 minus $23,000)]
   - 20% times ($502,000) equals $100,400
3) The Wage and Asset Limitation, which is the Greater value of:
   - 50% of the employee Wages the business paid
     - 50% times $150,000 in Wages equals $75,000
   - (25% of the Wages) + (2.5% of the UBIA of the Business Assets)
     - 25% times $150,000 in Wages equals $37,500
     - 2.5% times $200,000 of the UBIA Assets equals $5,000
     - $37,500 plus $5,000 equals $42,500
   - The Greater of these two values is $75,000

The Final Line 9 Qualified Business Income Deduction is $75,000
This is the lesser value of:
   The Normal QBI Deduction of $87,203 or
   The Taxable Income Limitation of $100,400 or

   The Wage and Asset Limitation of $75,000

In this Example #2, the final QBI Deduction is limited by the amount of W-2 Wages paid to the Plumber's four employees, in this case the 50% of the total $150,000 of Wages valued at $75,000.

When the Taxable Income is above the Taxable Income phase-out levels, this business must have Wages or Assets, to benefit from the QBI Deduction. They would get no deduction if there were no Wages or Assets.

In practice this is usually not an issue, as the business typically needs employees and business assets to create the final Taxable Income above the phase-out values. It is generally difficult to create this level of Qualified Business Income without employees, equipment, and assets.

The top of the Taxable Income phase-out levels again are:
- Above $415,000 for a Married Filing Jointly couple
- Above $207,500 for Unmarried or Married Filing Separately individuals

Example #3: The Sole Proprietor Plumber where their Married Filing Jointly combined Taxable Income is **Between** the phase-out range between $315,000 up to $415,000 for their Married Filing Jointly status.
The Facts of the Example:

Since the Taxable Income is **Between** the phase-out levels, the Wage and Asset Limitation "effect" is pro-rated down from the full amount. You will see this in the calculations.
1) The Plumber files as Married Filing Jointly with his wife
2) Their combined Taxable Income before QBI deduction is $385,000
   • Including $23,000 of Net Capital Gain
3) Their Taxable Income is **Between** the $315,000 to $415,000 values of the Taxable Income phase-out levels.
4) The Plumber's business showed a $250,000 net profit for the year
   • He has a deduction of $11,309 of 1/2 of his self-employment tax
5) The Plumber is considered to be a "Qualified Trade or Business", not the more restrictive "Specified Service Trade or Business" SSTB.
6) The Plumber had no deductions for self-employed health insurance or for a contribution to a self-employed retirement plan
7) The Plumber has two employees as apprentice plumbers
   • The Plumber paid $85,000 in W-2 Wages to these two employees
8) The Plumber has three pickup trucks and plumbing tools as Assets
   • The UBIA (Unadjusted Basis Immediately after Acquisition) of the three trucks and plumbing tools is $150,000

The Rules to Calculate this Qualified Business Income (QBI) Deduction:
1) The QBI Deduction will be the lower of these two values
   • The "Reduced" Normal QBI Deduction
     • 20% of Qualified Business Income minus the Reduction Amount
       • The Reduction Amount is the difference between the higher Normal QBI Deduction and the lower Wage and Asset Limitation, multiplied then by a Reduction Ratio value.
   • The Taxable Income Limitation
     • 20% of [(Taxable Income) minus (Net Capital Gain)]

The Calculations:
1) The Normal QBI Deduction
   • 20% of his [(Qualified Business Income)]
   • 20% of his [(Net Business Profit) minus (1/2 SE Tax)]
   • 20% times [($250,000) minus ($11,309)]
   • 20% times $238,691 equals $47,738

2) The Taxable Income Limitation
   - 20% of their [(Taxable Income) minus (Net Capital Gain)]
   - 20% times [($385,000 minus $23,000)]
   - 20% times ($362,000) equals $72,400

3) The Wage and Asset Limitation, which is the Greater value of:
   - 50% of the employee Wages the business paid
     - 50% times $85,000 in Wages equals $42,500
   - (25% of the Wages) + (2.5% of the UBIA of the business Assets)
     - 25% times $85,000 equals $21,250
     - 2.5% times $150,000 of the UBIA Assets equals $3,750
     - $21,250 plus $3,750 equals $25,000
   - The Greater of these two values is $42,500

4) Calculate the Excess Amount - as the Difference between the higher Normal QBI Deduction and the lower Wage and Asset Limitation:
   - The Normal QBI Deduction is $47,738
   - The Wage and Asset Limitation is $42,500
   - The difference between these two values is the Excess Amount:
     - $47,738 minus $42,500 equals $5,238

5) The Reduction Ratio is calculated as follows:
   - What is the amount of Taxable Income above the lower limit?
     - $385,000 minus $315,000 equals $70,000
   - What is the difference between the phase-out levels of $315,000 to $415,000? That is $100,000.
   - What percentage is the Taxable Income into the phase-out level?
     - $70,000 divided by $100,000 equals 70% = the Reduction Ratio

6) Calculate the Reduction Amount as follows:
   - The difference between the Normal QBI Deduction and the Wage and Asset Limitation equals $5,238 as calculated in Step 4 above.
   - This Excess Amount times the Reduction Ratio equals:
     - $5,238 times 70% equals $3,667 = the Reduction Amount

7) Calculate the "Reduced" Normal QBI Deduction as follows:
   - The Normal QBI Deduction minus the Reduction Amount
   - $47,738 minus $3,667 equals $44,071

The Final Line 9 Qualified Business Income Deduction is $44,071

This is the lesser value of:

The "Reduced" Normal QBI Deduction of $44,071 or
The Taxable Income Limitation of $72,400

In this Example #3, the final QBI Deduction is pro-rated down by 70% of the $5,238 value Between the higher Normal QBI Deduction of $47,738 to the lower Wage and Asset Limitation of $42,500.

This is the main difference between the previous Example #2 where the Taxable Income was **Above** the phase-out range therefore with the full-value Wage and Asset Limitation in effect - and this Example #3 where the Taxable Income was **Between** the phase-out range, which then pro-rates down the effect of the full-value Wage and Asset Limitation.

It is very logical and fair when you consider how the IRS designed this.

If the Taxable Income is **Above** the phase-out range, you are limited by the full value of the Wage and Asset limitation, if that value is below your Normal QBI Deduction value.

If the Taxable Income is **Between** the phase-out range, you are only partially limited by the full value of the Wage and Asset limitation, if that value is below your Normal QBI Deduction value.

Congress designed this QBI deduction to give a tax deduction incentive to the unincorporated small businesses that have the earning capacity to hire employees. A "Qualified Trade or Business" like the Plumber, when over the Taxable Income upper threshold for his filing status, will get no QBI deduction if he does not hire employees he pays W-2 wages to, and/or he has no depreciable assets used in his business. If the Plumber only had assets and no employees, his QBI deduction would be very small. You will see in example #5, that an SSTB business owner gets no QBI deduction when they are over the Taxable Income upper threshold.

Of course, as always, the tax software will interview you to get the QBI business facts, then it will calculate the correct QBI Deduction. It is very useful, though, to understand the calculations. Then you can be confident you received the correct QBI Deduction for your business.

Example #4: A wife of a married couple who operates a Sole Proprietor Accounting business. Her combined Taxable Income with her husband is **Below** the phase-out range between $315,000 up to $415,000 for their Married Filing Jointly status. She can benefit from a full QBI Deduction.

The Facts of the Example:
1) The Accountant files as Married Filing Jointly with her husband
2) Their combined Taxable Income before QBI deduction is $215,000
   • Including $88,000 of Net Capital Gain
3) Their Taxable Income is **Below** the $315,000 lower value of the Taxable Income phase-out levels between $315,000 to $415,000
4) The Accountant's business showed a $145,000 net profit for the year
   • She has a deduction of $9,903 of 1/2 of her self-employment tax
5) The Accountant is considered to be the more restrictive "Specified Service Trade or Business" SSTB.
6) They receive their family health insurance through her husband's job
7) The Accountant did not contribute to a self-employed retirement plan

The Rules to Calculate this Qualified Business Income (QBI) Deduction:
1) The QBI Deduction will be the <u>lower</u> of these two values
   • The Normal QBI Deduction
     • 20% of her [(Qualified Business Income)]
     • 20% of her [(Net Business Profit) minus (1/2 SE Tax)]
   • The Taxable Income Limitation
     • 20% of their [(Taxable Income) minus (Net Capital Gain)]

The Calculations:
1) The Normal QBI Deduction
   • 20% of her [(Qualified Business Income)]
   • 20% of her [(Net Business Profit) minus (1/2 SE Tax)]
   • 20% times [($145,000) minus ($9,903)]
   • 20% times $135,097 equals <u>$27,019</u>
2) The Taxable Income Limitation
   • 20% of their [(Taxable Income) minus (Net Capital Gain)]
   • 20% times [($215,000 minus $88,000)]
   • 20% times ($127,000) equals <u>$25,400</u>

The Final Line 9 Qualified Business Income Deduction is $25,400
This is the <u>lesser</u> value of:
   The Normal QBI Deduction of <u>$27,019</u> or
   The Taxable Income Limitation of <u>$25,400</u>

Example #5: A wife of a married couple who operates a Sole Proprietor Accounting business. Her combined Taxable Income with her husband is **Above** the phase-out range between $315,000 up to $415,000 for their Married Filing Jointly status.

Her Accounting firm is a "Specified Service Trade or Business" SSTB.

An SSTB business **does not** receive any QBI deduction when their Taxable Income is **Above** the income phase-out levels for their filing status.

See this IRS Article that explains this limitation and other QBI FAQs:
https://www.irs.gov/newsroom/tax-cuts-and-jobs-act-provision-11011-section-199a-qualified-business-income-deduction-faqs

Congress wanted to limit the potential misuse by some of these Pass-Through, Sole Proprietor or Single-Member LLC business entities, to unduly benefit from this new 20% QBI Deduction. They did not want individual Personal Service Professionals converting their high-salaried personal service income into self-employed Qualified Business Income, just to then qualify for the new QBI Deduction. The QBI Deduction was intended for unincorporated small business owners that can hire workers.

For Example:
A high-earner General Surgeon who is salaried as an employee of a hospital, switching to create a Single-Member LLC business that would then just bill the same hospital as a self-employed surgeon for his/her same services. Congress did not want to encourage high-earner salaried professional workers to switch to being "self-employed" just to then be able to benefit from this 20% Qualified Business Income deduction.

Therefore Congress designated these Professional Service job categories with the label "Specified Service Trade or Business" SSTB in the Professions where they felt the most potential for misuse might occur. The denial of the QBI Deduction above the Taxable Income phase-out levels was the solution Congress created to stem the misuse they anticipated might occur by Professionals switching from being salaried to be self-employed. There is even a question in the tax software for the 2018 tax returns to ask if this new QBI income was from a former employer. The IRS could Audit taxpayers to observe their QBI compliance, to prevent such switching from high-income salary wages to being self-employed.

Example #6: A wife of a married couple who operates a Sole Proprietor Accounting business. Her combined Taxable Income with her husband is **Between** the phase-out range between $315,000 up to $415,000 for their Married Filing Jointly status. She will partially benefit from the QBI Deduction. This example is similar to Example #3, with one additional restriction because she is an SSTB business.

The Facts of the Example:

Since the Taxable Income is **Between** the phase-out levels, the Wage and Asset Limitation "effect" is pro-rated down from the full amount. In addition the values used in the calculations for the Qualified Business Income, the W-2 Employee Wages, and the UBIA value of the Business Assets are also pro-rated down. This is called the Applicable Percentage Reduction of these three values. You will see this in the calculations.
1) The Accountant files as Married Filing Jointly with her husband
2) Their combined Taxable Income before QBI deduction is $355,000
    • Including $28,000 of Net Capital Gain
3) Their Taxable Income is **Between** the $315,000 to $415,000 values of the Taxable Income phase-out levels.
4) The Accountant's business showed a $295,000 net profit for the year
    • She has a deduction of $11,911 of 1/2 of her self-employment tax
5) The Accountant had no deductions for self-employed health insurance or for a contribution to a self-employed retirement plan
6) The Accountant is considered to be the more restrictive "Specified Service Trade or Business" SSTB.
7) The Accountant has two employees as a bookkeeper and a secretary
    • The Accountant pays $100,000 in W-2 Wages to the 2 employees
8) The Accountant has computers and office furniture as Assets
    • The UBIA (Unadjusted Basis Immediately after Acquisition) of the computers and office furniture is $75,000

The Rules to Calculate this Qualified Business Income (QBI) Deduction:
1) The QBI Deduction will be the lower of these two values
    • The "Reduced" Normal QBI Deduction
        • 20% of Qualified Business Income minus the Reduction Amount
            • The Reduction Amount is the difference between the higher Normal QBI Deduction and the lower Wage and Asset Limitation, multiplied then by a Reduction Ratio value.
    • The Taxable Income Limitation
        • 20% of [(Taxable Income) minus (Net Capital Gain)]

The Calculations:

1) <u>The Applicable Percentage Reduction Value calculation is as follows:</u>
   - This is the reduction percentage value that will be used to reduce:
     - The original Qualified Business Income
     - The original employee W-2 Wages paid
     - The original UBIA value of the Business Assets
   - How much is the Taxable Income above the lower threshold?
     - Their Taxable Income is $355,000 before any QBI deduction
     - The lower threshold value is $315,000
     - ($355,000 minus $315,000) equals $40,000
   - What is the difference between the higher/lower thresholds?
     - $415,000 minus $315,000 equals $100,000
   - $40,000 divided by $100,000 equals 40%.
     - Therefore they are 40% into the phase-out threshold levels
   - The Applicable Percentage Reduction Value is 100% minus how far their Taxable Income is into the phase-out levels.
     - 100% minus 40% equals 60%
   - Therefore they can use 60% of these values for the calculations:
     - The original value of the Qualified Business Income is $283,089
       - [(Net Business Profit) minus (1/2 SE Tax)]
       - $295,000 minus $11,911 equals $283,089
     - The original value of the employee W-2 Wages paid is $100,000
     - The original value of the UBIA Business Assets is $75,000

2) <u>The Reduced Calculation values using the 60% Applicable Percentage:</u>
   - <u>The Qualified Business Income</u> - reduction down from $283,089
     - $283,089 times 60% equals **$169,853** (the reduced value)
     - Use <u>$169,853</u> for Qualified Business Income in the calculations
   - <u>The employee W-2 Wages paid</u> - reduction down from $100,000
     - $100,000 times 60% equals **$60,000** (the reduced value)
     - Use <u>$60,000</u> for the employee Wages in the calculations
   - <u>The UBIA value of the Business Assets</u> - down from $75,000
     - $75,000 times 60% equals **$45,000** (the reduced value)
     - Use <u>$45,000</u> for the UBIA Assets value in the calculations

3) <u>The Normal QBI Deduction</u>
   - 20% of her "reduced" Qualified Business Income
   - 20% times $169,853 equals <u>$33,971</u>

4) The Taxable Income Limitation
   - 20% of their [(Taxable Income) minus (Net Capital Gain)]
   - 20% times [($355,000 minus $28,000)]
   - 20% times ($327,000) equals $65,400

5) The Wage and Asset Limitation, which is the Greater of:
   - 50% of the "reduced" employee Wages the business paid
     - 50% times $60,000 of the "reduced" Wages equals $30,000
   - (25% of "reduced" Wages) + (2.5% of the "reduced" UBIA Assets)
     - 25% times $60,000 of the "reduced" Wages equals $15,000
     - 2.5% times $45,000 of the "reduced" UBIA Assets equals $1,125
     - $15,000 plus $1,125 equals $16,125
   - The Greater of these two values is $30,000

6) Calculate the Excess Amount - as The Difference between the higher Normal QBI Deduction and the lower Wage and Asset Limitation:
   - The Normal QBI Deduction is $33,971
   - The Wage & Asset Limitation is $30,000
   - The difference between these two values is the Excess Amount:
     - $33,971 minus $30,000 equals $3,971

7) The Reduction Ratio is calculated as follows:
   - What is the amount of Taxable Income above the lower limit?
     - $355,000 minus $315,000 equals $40,000
   - What is the difference between the phase-out levels of $315,000 to $415,000. That is $100,000.
   - What percentage is the Taxable Income into the phase-out level?
     - $40,000 divided by $100,000 equals 40% - the Reduction Ratio

8) Calculate the Reduction Amount as follows:
   - The difference between the Normal QBI Deduction and the Wage and Asset Limitation equals $3,971 as calculated in Step 6 above.
   - $3,971 times The Reduction Ratio equals the Reduction Amount
     - $3,971 times 40% equals $1,588

9) Calculate the "Reduced" Normal QBI Deduction as follows:
   - The Normal QBI Deduction minus the Reduction Amount
   - $33,971 minus $1,588 equals $32,383

The Final Line 9 Qualified Business Income Deduction is $32,383

This is the lesser value of:

The "Reduced" Normal QBI Deduction of $32,383 or
The Taxable Income Limitation of $65,400

This Example #6 is by far the most complicated QBI calculation for a Sole Proprietor individual who also is an SSTB business type.

To review: here is the logic of the IRS calculations for this Example #6:
1) The Accountant is a "Specified Service Trade or Business" SSTB
2) Taxable Income is **Between** the MFJ phase-out levels, therefore
3) An SSTB must use the Applicable Percentage to initially reduce:
    1) The Qualified Business Income
    2) The employee W-2 Wages the business paid
    3) The UBIA (Unadjusted Basis Immediately after Acquisition) Assets
4) These "reduced" values are then used to calculate the:
    1) The higher Normal QBI Deduction
    2) The lower Wage and Asset Limitation
5) Calculate the difference between these two values as Excess Amount
6) Calculate the Reduction Ratio of Taxable Income into the threshold
7) Calculate then the Reduction Amount value
8) Subtract the Reduction Amount from the Normal QBI Deduction
9) Use the lesser of the "Reduced" Normal QBI Deduction or the Taxable Income Limitation values

The IRS added the Applicable Percentage Reduction calculations to an SSTB entity with Taxable Income **Between** the income thresholds, to coordinate with the fact that an SSTB gets no QBI Deduction if their Taxable Income is **Above** the upper level of these phase-out values.

The worksheets to calculate these "Complex" QBI deductions are in the Publication 535 - Business Expenses, pages 49 - 57.
See that IRS link at:
https://www.irs.gov/pub/irs-pdf/p535.pdf

The Congress enacted the distinctions between the "Qualified Trade or Business" like the Plumber, as compared to a "Specified Service Trade or Business" like the Accountant. The IRS in turn has solved how to handle these six situations with their described definitions and calculations.

Qualified Business Income Deduction - Online Calculator

You can use this online QBI Deduction calculator to verify the calculations in these six examples and for your own tax return scenarios. See the link below and the screen shot of the QBI Calculator screen.

https://bradfordtaxinstitute.com/Tools/199A-Calculator/

199A Deduction Calculator

Enter Information		
Single or Married	Married	Enter, then tab to next cell
Taxable Income	375,000	
Net Capital Gains	100,000	
Qualified Business Income (QBI)	250,000	For definition of qualified business income see Tax Reform, New Item 20 Percent Deduction for Business income
Specified Service Business?	No	
Wages Paid by Business	0	
Qualified Property in Business	0	For definition of qualified property see Tax Reform, New Item 20 Percent Deduction for Business Property

Results	
Your 199A Deduction:	$20,000

Calculation Details

Use This Calculation		
Calculation if Below Phaseout Range	Calculation for Non-Service Business if in Phaseout Range	Calculation for Specified Service Business if in Phaseout Range
Lesser of	20% of QBI $50,000	20% of QBI (multiplied by applicable percentage) $20,000 TRUE 0.4
20% of QBI $50,000	Greater of Wage and Asset $0	Greater of Wage and Asset (multiplied by applicable percentage) $0
20% of Defined Taxable Income $55,000	Difference Between QBI and Greater of Wages/Assets $50,000	Difference Between QBI and Greater of Wages/Assets $20,000
Deduction Limit $50,000	Reduction to QBI $30,000	Reduction to QBI $12,000
* Defined Taxable = Taxable Income - Net Capital Gains	Phaseout Deduction $20,000	Phaseout Deduction $8,000
	Calculation for Non-Service Business Above Phaseout	Calculation for Specified Service Business if Phased Out
	20% of QBI (or Defined Taxable Income if lower) $50,000	No Deduction Allowed 0
	50% of Wages $0	
	25% of Wages $0	
	2.5% of Assets $0	
	Greater of 50% Wages vs. 25% Wages & Assets $0	
	Lesser of QBI (or Defined Taxable Income) and Wage/Asset $0	

Copyright © 2018/2019 by W. Murray Bradford, CPA

The 2018 Qualified Business Income loss carryover to 2019

If your Qualified Business had a net loss in 2018 you will receive no QBI deduction - as you will have no positive Qualified Business Income to use in the QBI Calculations. That QBI loss value will carryover to the 2019 tax year to reduce any 2019 Qualified Business Income calculation.

For Example:

1) Let's assume your Sole Proprietor Plumbing business for the 2018 tax year showed a $10,000 loss. You would receive no QBI deduction on your 2018 tax return. You now have a $10,000 QBI loss carryover.
2) The 2019 tax year was much more profitable for you, such that your Qualified Business Income for 2019 was $75,000.
3) Your 2019 net Qualified Business Income would be:
   1) $75,000 profit (2019) minus $10,000 loss (2018) equals $65,000
4) Your 2019 simple Normal QBI Deduction would be:
   1) 20% times $65,000 equals $13,000

This is a simplified example, as it does not take into consideration the deductions for 1/2 of the self-employment tax, self-employed health insurance paid, or contributions to a self-employed retirement plan.

Chapter 9:

Small Business Deductions and Bonus Tax changes

TOPICS SUMMARY #38 to #41

38) <u>More generous Depreciation rules for Small Business</u>

- The Bonus Depreciation now allows a 100% first-year deduction. Used, as well as new property, can benefit from this deduction.
- The Section 179 Expense deduction was doubled to up to $1 million
- The Business Depreciation Auto Limits were tripled
- Computers and Peripheral Equipment were removed from the definition of Listed Property, so the business use substantiation requirements are now not as restrictive for this equipment type use.

39) <u>Meals and Entertainment deduction changes for Small Business</u>

Client Entertainment Expenses for these small business owners are no longer allowed as a deduction. The business meal deduction rules have also changed slightly.

40) <u>Like-Kind Exchange rule changes for Small Business</u>

Like-Kind Exchanges in the tax year 2018 and beyond, are now limited to Real Property (Real Estate) not held primarily for sale. The Real Property must be used in a trade or business - such as a warehouse, or for an investment - such as a rental property.

41) <u>The tax withholding rate on Bonuses for the 2018 tax year is 22% compared to 25% previously</u>

Supplemental Wages and Bonuses will now be subject to a tax withholding rate of 22% in 2018 and beyond – provided the Bonus is under $1 million.

38) More generous Depreciation rules for Small Business

Bonus Depreciation now allows for the 100% first-year deduction for property acquired and placed in service after 09/27/2017 and before 01/01/2023. Used property now qualifies, in addition to new property.

The Section 179 Expense deduction was doubled to up to $1 million from the 2017 value of $500,000. The phase-out threshold is now $2.5 million. Section 179 qualified real property used in business now includes:
- Personal property used predominately to furnish lodging
- Roofs, HVAC property, fire protection, alarm and security systems.

Business Depreciation Auto Limits have tripled for passenger vehicles, trucks and vans placed in service after 12-31-2017, for which Bonus Depreciation was not claimed. Refer to the table below. See this article from the Iowa State University-Center for Agricultural Law & Taxation. https://www.calt.iastate.edu/blogpost/looking-vehicle-depreciation-and-expensing-under-new-tax-law

Depreciation Tables based on tables in TheTaxBook™, redrawn by the Author for clarity.

Vehicle Depreciation Limitations (Section 280F)				
Tax Year First Placed in Service	2018*	2017	2016	2015
Auto Depreciation Limitations Based on 100% Business or Investment Use:				
1st Year if Special Depreciation is Claimed	$18,000	$11,160	$11,160	$11,160
1st Year Depreciation	$10,000	$3,160	$3,160	$3,160
2nd Year Depreciation	$16,000	$5,100	$5,100	$5,100
3rd Year Depreciation	$9,600	$3,050	$3,050	$3,050
Each Suceeding Year	$5,760	$1,875	$1,875	$1,875
Trucks and Vans Depreciation Limitations Based on 100% Business or Investment Use. (Same as Autos for Years after 2017)				
1st Year if Special Depreciation is Claimed	$18,000	$11,560	$11,560	$11,460
1st Year Depreciation	$10,000	$3,560	$3,560	$3,460
2nd Year Depreciation	$16,000	$5,700	$5,700	$5,600
3rd Year Depreciation	$9,600	$3,450	$3,350	$3,350
Each Suceeding Year	$5,760	$2,075	$2,075	$1,975
* Vehicles Acquired after September 27th, 2017, and Placed In Service During 2018.				

Computers and Peripheral Equipment were removed from the definition as being considered Listed Property, so the business use substantiation requirements are not as restrictive for these computer equipment uses.

39) Meals and Entertainment deduction changes for Small Business

Client Entertainment expenses for small business owners are no longer allowed as a deduction. This is a permanent change. In recent tax years you could deduct 50% of the cost of entertainment expenses such as:
- Sporting events, theater tickets, golf outings, etc.
- 100% of the cost of qualified charitable events, if the purpose was business related
- Company sponsored Office Holiday Parties are still 100% deductible

50% of Employee Travel Meals/Client Business Meals are still deductible:
- Including meals provided for the convenience of the employer
  - For instance the dinners provided for your employees working overtime one evening

See the table, blog article and IRS publications below:

Deduction Tables based on blog by Hertzback & Company, P.A. – Accountants redrawn by the Author for clarity.

Expense Category	2017 Expenses (Old Rules)	2018 Expenses (New Rules)
Office Holiday Parties	100% Deductible	100% Deductible
Entertaining Clients	50% Deductible	No Deduction for Entertainmen Expenses
	Event Tickets, 50% Deductible for Face Value of Ticket. Anything above Face Value is Non-Deductible.	
	Tickets to Qualified Charitable Events are 100% Deductible	
Business Meals e.g. Meals w/ Clients & Employee Travel Meals	50% Deductible	50% Deductible
Meals Provided for the Convenience of the Employer	100% Deductible Provided they are Excludible from Employee's income as De Minimis Fringe Benefits. Otherwise, 50% Deductible	50% Deductible (Non-Deductible after 2025)

https://www.hertzbach.com/2017/12/meals-and-entertainment-changes-under-tax-reform/

IRS Publication 535-Business Expenses explains what expenses are allowed and which are not. Publication 334 is a tax guide for Small Business. Publication 463 covers Travel, Gift, and Car expenses.
See the IRS links below to these three publications.
https://www.irs.gov/pub/irs-pdf/p535.pdf
https://www.irs.gov/pub/irs-pdf/p334.pdf
https://www.irs.gov/pub/irs-pdf/p463.pdf

40) Like-Kind Exchange rule changes
for Small Business

The 2018 tax year and beyond Like-Kind Exchanges are now limited to only Real Property (Real Estate). This is a permanent change in the law.

Like-Kind Exchange rules quoted below from IRS Fact Sheet (FS-2008-18)
https://www.irs.gov/pub/irs-news/fs-08-18.pdf

* *

"Whenever you sell business or investment property and you have a gain, you generally have to pay tax on the gain at the time of sale.

Internal Revenue Code (IRC) Section 1031 provides an exception and allows you to postpone paying tax on the gain if you reinvest the proceeds in similar property as part of a qualifying Like-Kind exchange. Gain deferred in a Like-Kind exchange under IRC Section 1031 is tax-deferred, but it is not tax-free.

The exchange can include like-kind property exclusively or it can include like-kind property along with cash, liabilities and property that are not like-kind. If you receive cash, relief from debt(s), or property that is not like-kind, however, you may trigger some taxable gain in the year of the exchange. This will be reported on that current year's tax return.

There can be both deferred and recognized gain in the same transaction when a taxpayer exchanges for like-kind property of lesser value.

Both properties must be held for use in a trade or business or for investment. Property used primarily for personal use, like a primary residence or a second home or vacation home, does not qualify for like-kind exchange treatment."
* *

In the recent tax years previous to the 2018 tax year, other business or investment Personal Property, other than just Real Property, could be exchanged using the above Like-Kind Exchange rules. An example would have been farm Personal Property used as business property on a farm.
- An older Ford pickup truck exchanged for a similar used Chevy pickup truck
- A farm tractor exchanged for a wheat combine
- A single walk-in milking machine exchanged for a portable milking machine

The old Like-Kind Exchange rules were still in effect if you disposed of the business or investment related Personal Property on or before December 31st, 2017, or if the replacement business or investment related Personal Property was received on or before December 31st, 2017

Like-Kind Exchanges in the tax years 2018 and beyond, are now limited to only Real Property not held primarily for sale.
- In other words, non-inventory real estate
- Real Property used only in a business or for investment purposes

The major 2018 tax law change to IRC Section 1031 is the complete repeal of Personal Property Like-Kind Exchanges. The IRC Code Section 1031 now refers exclusively to Real Property assets, and has been retitled, "Exchange of Real Property held for productive use or investment." See the IRC Code Section 1031 at:
https://www.law.cornell.edu/uscode/text/26/1031
See the IRS articles below:
"Like-Kind Exchanges now limited to real property"
https://www.irs.gov/newsroom/like-kind-exchanges-now-limited-to-real-property
"Like-Kind Exchanges - Real Estate Tax Tips"
https://www.irs.gov/businesses/small-businesses-self-employed/like-kind-exchanges-real-estate-tax-tips

41) Bonuses now subject to a 22% tax withholding rate compared to 25% previously

The tax withholding rate on Supplemental Wages, like Bonuses – has been reduced to 22% in the tax year 2018. This is a permanent change. Supplemental wages were subject to a 25% tax withholding rate in 2017 and recent tax years. They will now be subject to a flat 22% withholding rate in 2018 and beyond – provided the bonus is under $1 million. The rate stays at 22% until changed by the IRS for future tax years. See page 2 of this IRS Notice 1036 for the 22% tax withholding rate at:
https://www.irs.gov/pub/irs-pdf/n1036.pdf

Bio of the Author

Who is Michael D. Meyer, EA
and
Why is He Qualified to Write a Book about Taxes

My Personal History

I grew up in a small town in southeastern Indiana called Lawrenceburg, graduating from high school in 1978. I graduated from the University of Notre Dame in 1983 with a 5-year degree in Architecture. My 3rd year of college I lived and studied abroad in Rome, Italy – participating in the ND Rome Studies Program for their Architectural students.

I moved to New York City in October of 1985, and married a Jersey Girl, Michele, in September 1987. We recently celebrated 32 years together. We both love New York City – to us the greatest city in the world!

I worked for many decades in Architecture and Construction until the 2008 market crash, when I decided to pursue a second recession-proof career in tax preparation. The work for Architects and Contractors often slows during recessions, so I created a backup career. I retired from Architecture in April 2018, to concentrate all my efforts running my small Tax Practice, and becoming a more experienced Enrolled Agent.

Tax Preparation Professional Development - at H&R Block (2012 to 2017)

I took the H&R Block Income Tax Course in the Fall of 2012 and soon after passed the IRS exam to become a Registered Tax Return Preparer (RTRP) in November 2012. The RTRP was the IRS certified designation offered at that time for tax preparers who were not Enrolled Agents.

I then worked as a seasonal Tax Professional for H&R Block for four years. I attained the status of Master Tax Advisor within H&R Block, their highest tax professional certification level at that time.

I was given the privilege to complete well over 700 paid tax returns for H&R Block clients during my four-year tenure with the company as a seasonal tax professional.

<u>Professional Development: Enrolled Agent and NTPI Fellow (2016 to 2018)</u>

I became a licensed IRS Enrolled Agent (EA) in October 2016, and have been a member of the National Association of Enrolled Agents (NAEA) since November 2016. I attend the monthly meetings of the Metro Chapter of the New York State Society of Enrolled Agents, of which I am also a member. I am required to complete 30 hours/year of continuing education courses to maintain my EA status with the IRS and the NAEA. Enrolled Agents study the subjects of Professional Ethics, Federal Tax Updates, Federal Tax Law, and Representation Practice Procedures before the IRS, to satisfy their yearly continuing education requirements.

An Enrolled Agent (EA) is a person who has earned the privilege of practicing (that is, representing taxpayers) before the Internal Revenue Service. Enrolled Agents, like Attorneys (JDs) and Certified Public Accountants (CPAs), are unrestricted as to which taxpayers they can represent, what types of tax matters they can handle, and which IRS offices they can practice before. Enrolled Agents are licensed by the IRS within the U.S. Treasury Department, which is a Federal jurisdiction, which therefore allows an individual EA to practice in all 50 States.

In April 2018 I began the process to become an NTPI Fellow by November 2018, bestowed by the National Tax Practice Institute™ (NTPI). The NTPI Fellow curriculum is managed and administered by the NAEA.

NTPI Fellows are considered the experts in representing taxpayers before the IRS, with Examination, Audit, Collection, Payment Agreement, and Appeals tax matters. NTPI Fellows can legally represent Clients before the IRS, and act as an intermediary on the Client's behalf, so the Client does not have to deal with or speak with the IRS directly. Only credentialed tax experts, being CPAs, Attorneys, or Enrolled Agents, can become NTPI Fellows. They also perform the same duties representing Clients to the State taxing authorities.

I completed the online NTPI Level 1 courses in late April 2018. I completed the in-person NTPI Level 2 courses at the NAEA National Convention in Las Vegas in early August 2018. I completed the in-person NTPI Level 3 courses in Orlando in early November 2018, at the Fall NAEA gathering. I was granted the status of NTPI Fellow at the graduation ceremony on November 9th, 2018 - after I completed the NTPI Level 3 courses. I began representing Taxpayers in November, 2018.

Small Tax Practice and TurboTaxLive™ Credentialed Tax Expert (2017-19)

I started my own small tax practice in May 2017. My focus for the next several years is only Individual taxes, and making that process clear for Taxpayers, so they understand every line on their tax return. For the 2018 and 2019 tax seasons, I worked with my existing and new tax clients in our Upper West Side neighborhood in New York City.

I also worked during the 2018/2019 tax seasons with the TurboTax™ tax and accounting software company Intuit, in my capacity as an IRS Enrolled Agent, as one of their remote Credentialed Tax Experts for their new TurboTaxLive™ online tax product. I provided phone and interactive online video Tax Advice and Tax Return Review – for over 1,900 online TurboTax™ Customers – throughout the United States and the World. I have used TurboTax™ for many decades, and began in May 2017 using their ProSeries™ professional tax software for my tax practice clients.

Why "Taxes Are Easy" for me

Since that first H&R Block tax class in 2012, the process of completing a tax return has come very easily for me. The tax laws and how they are expressed on a tax return, just make sense to me. I enjoy immensely helping Individual taxpayers "solve" their yearly tax scenario, whether in person with my own clients, or "virtually" through TurboTaxLive™.

Most adult-age U.S. Citizens, Green Card Holders, and Resident Aliens have a yearly obligation to file a U.S. Individual Income Tax Return to report their financial activity for that tax year, and pay any taxes owed, or collect a refund. To make that process easy, and even enjoyable, is my business purpose. Thank you for allowing me to help make the "Tax Cuts & Jobs Act" more understandable for your tax scenario.

The name Michael D. Meyer is my official personal name and business name registered with all the divisions of the IRS related to me being an IRS Enrolled Agent. The national and local chapters of the National Association of Enrolled Agents also lists me as Michael D. Meyer.

Most people just refer to me as Mike. You can email me at Mike@TaxesAreEasy.com

Three Future Book Titles in the "Taxes Are Easy" series

In my capacity as a Credentialed Tax Expert in 2019 for TurboTaxLive™ I helped 1,271 TurboTax™ customers with their tax issues. These were by far the three most requested tax topics for explanation. I plan to write future "Taxes Are Easy" books to address these tax topics.

1) Self-Employment, Contract Work and Freelancing Work
- Report self-employment income/expenses on the Schedule C (Form 1040)
- Distinguish between self-employment and Airbnb rental income
- What are the "Ordinary and Necessary" expense categories?
- Self-Employment losses and the IRS profit rule for 3 of the last 5 years
- How to account for Inventory in the Cost of Goods Sold section
- How to Depreciate assets that will last for more than one year
- How to calculate the Home Office deduction
- How to deduct expenses for a Vehicle used in your business
- How to calculate and make quarterly Estimated Tax Payments

2) Rental Properties
- Report rental property income/expenses on the Schedule E (Form 1040)
- What are the Vacation Home rules?
- When to report Airbnb income as a rental income activity
- What are the "Ordinary and Necessary" expense categories?
- How to Depreciate assets that last for more than one year
- How to "catch up" on the Depreciation of the rental property building if not taken previously, using the IRS Form 3115
- How to deduct expenses for a Vehicle used in your business
- What are the Passive Activity Loss / Carryover rules?
- How to convert a Personal Residence into a Rental Property
- How to convert a Rental Property back into a Personal Residence
- How to report the eventual Sale of the Rental Property

3) Employee Stock Options granted to you as an employee benefit
- How to keep track of the Employee Stock Options granted to you
- What are the different types of Employee Stock Options?
- How to calculate the Cost Basis of the Stock Options you received
- When can you sell the Stock Shares you were granted?
- What are Short-Term and Long-Term Capital Gains?

Please send me an email at Mike@TaxesAreEasy.com for your preference as to which book should be written next. If you can, give an example of why that particular book subject would be helpful to you. Or perhaps you have a different "great idea" for a tax topic book. Please also share that with me.

41 TCJA Topics Index

Testimonials from Reviewers - the Taxpayers

Testimonials of the Taxpayer reviewers will be shown here and on the Amazon page to encourage Taxpayers to buy the book, to get the same benefits as described in these Testimonials.

Sienna from California
"Easy to read. Everything is clearly stated and explained at length."

Eileen from New York
"All the new changes in the U.S. tax laws can be daunting to the average taxpayer. This timely reference book packs a lot of information that helps explain many of these changes. For me, the way the book is designed to be used is very helpful and user-friendly. The topics are organized in chapters that make this information clear and digestible.

I do use TurboTax™ to complete my taxes but having read this book, I feel as though I have a better grasp of how portions of the tax law have changed and why. Although the book is available as an electronic resource, I like to have the physical copy so that I can highlight specific relevant parts that apply to me now and in the future as circumstances change. Maybe some day I too will find that "Taxes Are Easy". This book is an excellent start."

Elizabeth from New Hampshire
"This is a wonderful little book that provides great detail and clarification of the many tax law changes that have occurred in the past couple of years. A very helpful book for forward planning and bringing attention to some significant changes to deductions every tax payer should be aware of."

Liz from Arizona
"I found this book easy to follow to help understand the many new tax law changes. Good resource for a small business owner or self-employed person for tax planning."

Testimonials from Reviewers - the Taxpayers

Angie from Indiana
"This is a must-read for everyone who wants to make sure they are taking all the deductions available and to ensure they are keeping everything organized should they need to supply proof to the IRS.

As a Mortgage Loan Officer I found this book filled with valuable information which will not only help me personally but also my clients. Thank you for presenting the information in such an understandable format. I learned a lot! Especially about the Home Equity account deductions!

I would recommend this book to everyone! I really liked the book. I truly learned a lot and I amazed myself at all of the information that I didn't know! I think if everyone read this book they would start getting organized and ready for tax season a lot sooner! I also think they would maybe reconsider some of their financial decisions."

Joanne from Ohio
"For decades we have used tax consultants to file our tax returns. Despite having a PhD in Nursing, the tax law changes through the years seemed too complicated and political. Michael Meyer's booklet has enhanced the knowledge of our own tax scenario, to the point we will do our own taxes this upcoming year!"

Annie from New Jersey
"Take control with this in-depth and useful resource for the tax DIY enthusiast."

Testimonials from Reviewers - the Tax Professionals

Testimonials of Tax Professional reviewers will be shown here and on the Amazon page to encourage Tax Professionals to buy the book, to get the same benefits as described in these Testimonials.

Matthew, Tax Professional from New York

"As a tax preparer and office manager of a national retail tax office, the new 2018 tax laws have been a daily topic of conversation, and clients are pretty confused about the changes. Mike's book really gives you very clear explanations and talking points that make those discussions much easier to have.

Using this book will help preparers and clients alike, and will make preparations for the upcoming 2020 tax season much easier. I am also looking forward to the updated 2nd edition that will cover the 2019 forms and tax law changes."

Annetta, M.S., EA from New York

"I would like to express my sincere gratitude to Michael for taking the time to compose such a nicely written and thoughtfully organized "Tax Cuts and Jobs Act" book. This book is a valued contribution to our profession both as a handy resource and a guide to provide to clients for their betterment.

I would like to request that you consider writing a book on the Foreign Tax Credit and Foreign Earned Income Exclusion - the application of each and the coordination as well as inclusion of special situations for taxpayers abroad.

Additionally, I would choose to order your suggested future book titles in the order of 3/2/1 to work on in the future.

This book provides nice examples especially in regards to the revised Capital Gain Tax Rate Schedule and the Backdoor Roth IRA. The list of Acronyms is helpful and appreciated as well.

Thank you so much for sharing this book. I believe that the self-preparer as well as the tax preparer will find the material invaluable.

With Gratitude,
Annetta M.S. (Master of Science), EA (Enrolled Agent)
New York "

Notes

Notes

www.ingramcontent.com/pod-product-compliance
Lightning Source LLC
Chambersburg PA
CBHW060622200326
41521CB00007B/854